Essential Visual Basic 5.0 *Fast*
Includes ActiveX Control Development

Springer

London
Berlin
Heidelberg
New York
Barcelona
Budapest
Hong Kong
Milan
Paris
Santa Clara
Singapore
Tokyo

John Cowell

Essential Visual Basic 5.0 *Fast*

Includes ActiveX
Control Development

With 211 Figures

 Springer

John Cowell, BSc (Hons), MPhil, PhD
Department of Computer and Information Sciences
De Montfort University
Kents Hill Campus, Hammerwood Gate, Kents Hill
Milton Keynes, MK7 6HP, UK

ISBN 3-540-76148-9 Springer-Verlag Berlin Heidelberg New York

British Library Cataloguing in Publication Data
Cowell, John, 1957-
    EssentialVisual Basic 5.0 fast : includes ActiveX Control Development
    1.Visual Basic (Computer program language)   2.Visual
    programming (Computer science)
    I.Title
    005.1'33
ISBN 3540761489

Library of Congress Cataloging-in-Publication Data
    Cowell, John, 1957-
      Essential Visual Basic 5.0 fast : includes ActiveX Control
    Development / John Cowell.
          p.   cm.
      Includes index.
      ISBN 3-540-76148-9 (alk. paper)
        1. Application software- -development.   2. Microsoft Visual Basic.
      I. Title.
      QA76.76.A65C69   1997   97-17622
      005.26'8- -DC21   CIP

Typesetting: Camera ready by author
Printed and bound at the Athenæum Press Ltd., Gateshead, Tyne and Wear
34/3830-54321 Printed on acid-free paper

Contents

4 MANAGING PROJECTS AND FILES 30

5 STANDARD CONTROLS 37

6 BUYING A NEW PC.. 52

1

Why Use Visual Basic 5?

Introduction

Visual Basic 5 is the latest version of the best selling development environment from Microsoft. Visual Basic 4 set the standard for developers using Windows 95 and is the most popular way of creating professional Windows applications. Version 5 offers all the facilities of version 4 as well as a range of exciting new features. If you are developing software for the PC either as a professional programmer, a student, or for fun you will be working in a Windows 95 environment and if you are developing Windows 95 software you need Visual Basic 5.

Visual Basic has virtually become the industry standard for developing professional Windows applications with the minimum of fuss. It has rightly gained a reputation as a heavy-weight development environment which provides everything that a professional software developer could want in an affordable, friendly system. Visual Basic is a complete development environment, allowing complex applications to be developed with the minimum of programming. Many applications use databases and version 5 is now even better for developing database applications. ActiveX has become increasingly important and Visual Basic is one of the first tools that allows you to develop ActiveX controls and documents with the same ease as other Visual Basic Windows 95 applications.

The environment is very intuitive to use and if you already have some programming experience you can expect to use Visual Basic confidently after a few weeks practice with proficiency after about 2 months. If you have used a previous version of Visual Basic it will take even less time to make the change. Most experienced programmers find they prefer the Visual Basic environment to using languages such as C++. Inexperienced programmers who meet Visual Basic as their first language find it a great development environment and are often horrified if they later have to switch to another language which lacks the features and ease of use of Visual Basic.

There are now large numbers of companies offering additional OCX or ActiveX controls for Visual Basic, making it even easier for you to write your application. The chances are that whatever you want to do in a Windows 95 environment Visual Basic 5 will let you do it.

If you are a Delphi or Visual C++ programmer you can create ActiveX controls in Visual Basic and use them in these environments.

Why change to version 5?

Visual Basic version 4 was one of the best selling development environments of all time with a massive user base of over 4 million and was a hard act to follow. It was not easy to come up with a new version of Visual Basic which was not simply different but objectively better. Microsoft carried out extensive surveys of what its customers wanted from a new version, the four most commonly requested changes were:

- Improved performance.
- Ability to create and use ActiveX components.
- Better database access features.
- Improved programmer productivity.

Version 5 of Visual Basic addresses all of these issues. If you are currently using an earlier version of Visual Basic, it is worthwhile making the change to the latest version, since the changes are not just cosmetic, there are many things you can do in version 5 that you cannot do in earlier versions. Version 5 has an improved user interface and offers a range of new features which give you greater functionality. Visual Basic 5 uses object oriented terminology in all the supporting manuals and has new features that allow you to design object oriented software. For this reason alone it is worth making the switch to version 5. If you want to produce ActiveX controls or are serious about database development and Internet integration you need to use version 5.

Is this book for you?

This book is a complete revision for version 5 of Visual Basic and even if you are an existing Visual Basic user who wants to convert to the latest version, you will find this book is very helpful in giving a concise review of the key aspects of Visual Basic with emphasis on the latest features.

This book assumes that you have no prior knowledge of Visual Basic and provides an introduction to the language. It is also suitable for those at an intermediate level who want to learn how to develop serious, professional applications. It is assumed that you have some experience of using Windows programs such as word processors, spreadsheets and databases.

It is helpful if you already have some programming experience, but all the essential elements of the Visual Basic language are covered. If you have used BASIC before, especially variants such as QuickBASIC or QBasic, you will be able to switch to Visual Basic without any problems.

Visual Basic is supplied with manuals which are better than average and the usual high standard of on-line help. These are fine if you have a good grasp of Visual Basic and need to look up a specific point. What the manuals and help are not very good at is providing is a readable, impartial guide to the language and environment. This book does not cover every minor detail of Visual Basic in the same way as the manuals, but it does give you a grasp of all the most important features of the language. There are many illustrations and examples. The best way to learn Visual Basic is to try out the examples for yourself.

How this book is organised

This book can be used as a tutorial which you start at the beginning and work through to the end. If you do this, you will know enough to develop major applications. All the key concepts of programming in an object oriented environment are explained. If you already have some programming experience you will find that you do not have to read all of the chapters in depth, for example those dealing with the Visual Basic language. Many people have used one of the variants of BASIC such as QuickBASIC, but it is still worthwhile scanning the sections which deal with programming since each flavour of BASIC has its own peculiarities. This book is organised into chapters covering specific topics so that you can easily find the material you want.

If you already have some experience of Visual Basic, you can just concentrate on the chapters which deal with features you are interested in, such as databases or ActiveX control development. One of the key differences between this and earlier versions of Visual Basic is that there is an increasing emphasis on the object oriented approach to designing software. You can ignore the object oriented aspects of Visual Basic to a large extent, but if you want to be in line with the latest trends for developing software with fewer bugs, you do need to know about object orientation. One of the major growth areas in the past few years has been the increasing popularity of the World Wide Web. HTML is a language used for producing Web pages which are displayed in a browser such as Microsoft Explorer. ActiveX documents can be created in Visual Basic which can be displayed in the virtual environment provided by the browser.

The earlier parts of this book cover the organisation of projects, while later chapters cover more advanced topics such as creating and using ActiveX controls. This book is not intended to be a definitive in-depth description of Visual Basic - if it did it would be about ten times as long and take twenty times as long to read. The philosophy of this book is to cover a broad range of most of the key features of Visual Basic. Most people find that at first they don't need to learn everything about the language to be able to develop useful programs. If, for example, your first Visual Basic program does not use grids, you do not need to read the chapter on the custom controls in order to start. The best way to use this book is to read the chapters you need and to try the examples. One of the pleasures of Visual Basic is that it allows you to develop applications *fast* - you do not even need to read all of this book before you can start!

New features in version 5

This book is based on Version 5 - the latest version. Software developed using earlier revisions is compatible with this version. The main additional features that have been added are:

- Improved speed. One of the major problems with Visual Basic was that it was an interpreted language and applications ran slowly. This version offers a native compiler which offers a claimed improvement in performance of up to 20 times.
- There is improved speed of database access, up to 4 times is claimed. In particular asynchronous queries are supported.
- There are improved data access tools, including simplified database creation and queries.
- There is additional support for Windows NT, in particular multi-threading.
- Delivery and installation of applications via the Internet is supported.
- The Form Layout window allows you to specify where your form will appear on the screen when the application is run. This is useful if your form is not maximised when run and so does not occupy the entire screen.
- The **Decimal** data type has been introduced for increased accuracy.
- One of the most annoying features of any development environment where there are several windows open is that it is easy to lose windows. The menu bar has been changed so that you can display key windows, such as the toolbox and Properties window by clicking on an icon.
- The new Windows 97 style icons are used, which show the icon on a flat background rather than a pseudo button.
- There is a very noticeable change in the terminology used in Visual Basic 5, to support an object oriented design model. A button, for example, is referred to as an object, that is a member of the **CommandButton** class. While this does not indicate a change in the underlying philosophy of Visual Basic it does reflect the increasing use of object oriented design and implementation techniques.
- You can create ActiveX controls. These allow you to develop controls which can be used in other Visual Basic, Delphi or Visual C++ applications.
- An ActiveX Control Interface Wizard and a Property Pages Wizard have been added, to simplify the creation of ActiveX controls.
- The alignment controls for ensuring that objects on forms are correctly positioned have been greatly improved.
- You can now dock windows such as the toolbox rather than having them as independent windows.

- There is an on-line help facility available from the **Help** menu which connects to the Microsoft Web site.
- There are minor revisions to the programming language, including the introduction of enumerated types.
- There is an IntelliSense facility which offers you a list of alternative choices when typing code, for example when you type the name of an object, a list of all its properties is displayed.
- The Project Explorer is a new feature which allows you to find both code and objects in your project.

In addition, there are numerous changes to the user interfaces. The majority are improvements rather than just simply changes.

What computer do you need to run Visual Basic 5?

Computers are never fast enough and rarely have enough disk space or memory, so the faster and more powerful your computer the better. Microsoft suggest that an ideal development system for a professional Visual Basic programmer is:

- Intel Pentium P150.
- 64Mb of memory.
- 17" screen.
- 2Gb of disk space.

Realistically though, Visual Basic can be run with a more modest configuration and still provide reasonable performance. The minimum that you need so that the performance is adequate is:

- Intel 80486dx4 or better.
- 16MB or more of memory.
- 15" screen.
- 80 MB of disk space for a full installation.

Visual Basic runs satisfactorily with this configuration, but if you want to run other application at the same time there are improvements in speed if you have more than 16Mb of memory.

The Visual Basic 5 development environment requires you to have at least four or five windows open at the same time. Ideally you will need an SVGA screen, and even if you have excellent eyesight a monitor of 15 inches or more is a great help.

Versions of Visual Basic 5

Many people may still be using the Custom Control Edition (CCE) of Visual Basic 5 which is a surprisingly complete free version which may be downloaded from the Microsoft Web site. The only major omissions are that you cannot produce native compiled code and there are no database facilities, but there is enough in this free edition to introduce you to all the major features of this version.

There are three versions of the commercial release of the software:

- Learning. This is aimed primarily at the student market and does not include the native compiler, so it cannot be used for producing commercial applications for distribution to customers.
- Professional. This is a full implementation of the software and will be the version most widely used.
- Enterprise. Includes additional database support and tools for team working.

Conventions

There are a few conventions used in this book which make it easier to read:

- All program examples are in *italics*.
- All reserved words such as **For...Next** are in **bold** and start with a capital.
- Menu options are shown in **bold** as, for example, **View | Code** which means the **Code** option from the **View** menu.
- All user created identifiers such as *MyFile* are in italics.

2

The Visual Basic Environment

Introduction

This chapter describes the Visual Basic 5 environment. If you are a new user to Visual Basic, the initial reaction to seeing the development environment is one of confusion, but it is very clearly organised as you will see. If you have used earlier versions of Visual Basic some of the opening screens will seem familiar, but there are some significant improvements.

In this chapter you will learn about:

- Starting Visual Basic 5.
- Creating a shortcut to Visual Basic.
- The design form.
- The Project Explorer window.
- The Properties window.
- The menu bar.
- The toolbox window.

Starting Visual Basic 5

When you have installed Visual Basic you can run it from the taskbar as shown in fig 2.1.

- Click on **Start** on the taskbar.
- Click on **Programs**.
- Click on **Microsoft Visual Basic 5.0.**

•   Click on **Visual Basic 5.0**.

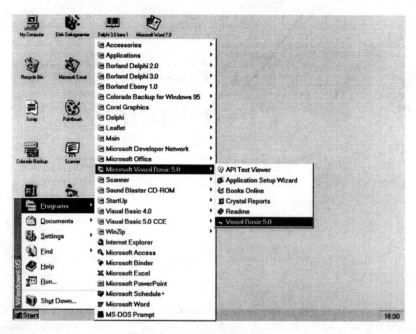

Fig 2.1 *Running Visual Basic.*

Since you are going to be running Visual Basic 5 a lot, a better way is to create a shortcut to it, so that you will simply have an icon on your desktop that you can click on to run it.

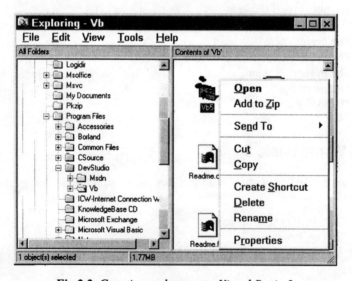

Fig 2.2 *Creating a shortcut to Visual Basic 5.*

To create a shortcut:

- Run the Windows Explorer.
- Find the Visual Basic 5 executable file, called vb5.exe. If you have chosen the default directories it will be in folder *C:\Program Files\DevStudio\VB*.
- When you have found this file, you can create a shortcut to it. Select the file and press the right mouse button.
- Select **Create Shortcut** from the speed menu as shown in fig 2.2.
- Finally drag the shortcut to your desktop, you will only be able to do this if the Windows Explorer form is not maximised.

If you cannot find this file, you can search for it using the search facility in the Windows Explorer:

- Run the Windows Explorer.
- Select the **Tools** menu item.
- Select the **Find** option.
- Select the **Files or Folders** option.
- Specify the name of the file VB5.EXE in the **Named** text box shown in fig 2.3.
- Specify C:\ in the **Look in** box. Make sure that you have checked the **Include subfolders** box.
- Click on the **Find Now** button to search the whole of your C: drive for the file.

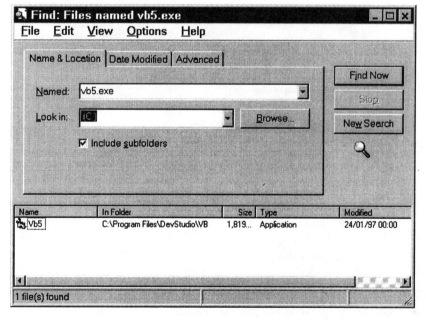

Fig 2.3 *Finding VB5.EXE.*

When the file has been found:

- Select it and right click on it to display the speed menu.
- Select the **Create Shortcut** option.
- Drag the Shortcut to your startup screen.

The Visual Basic design screen

When you start Visual Basic you have a choice of different applications that you can create as shown in fig 2.4. The most common type is the standard EXE.

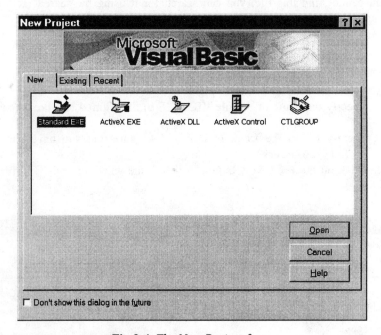

Fig 2.4 The New Project form.

The Visual Basic development environment is shown in fig 2.5. If you are new to visual development environments it is important to stay calm the first time that you see the Visual Basic 5 design screen. In a few hours all of the elements of the screen will seem very familiar. The screen has four windows

- The form. This is where you create the form that you are designing.
- The Form Layout window.
- The Properties window.
- The Project window.

There are three other important components to the design environment, which may not be displayed the first time you run Visual Basic:

- The menu bars.

- The toolbars.
- The toolbox.

design form   toolbar   menu bar

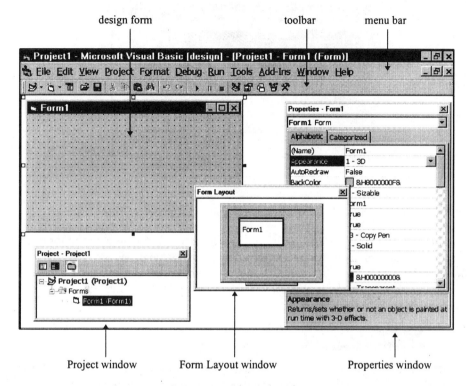

Project window   Form Layout window   Properties window

Fig 2.5 The Visual Basic 5 design screen.

The first time you run Visual Basic you will not see the toolbox. How you display and use the toolbox is covered later in this chapter.

The form

The main part of the design screen is the form, which will be similar to the one shown in fig 2.6.

If you are developing a Standard EXE or ActiveX control, it is likely that your application will include at least one form, since an application without a form cannot display any information to the user. Therefore Visual Basic 5 creates one form when an application is started. This form has the default heading of *Form1*. If you create a second form it will have the default name of *Form2* and so on. The naming sequence is logical but not imaginative. If you want to change it you can, however, if you do intend to change the name of a form, you should do so before you write any code for other controls that you put on the form. If you do change the name of a form after adding controls and writing some supporting Basic code, the application will not run correctly.

minimise/maximise

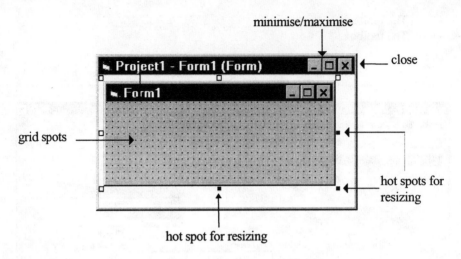

close

grid spots

hot spots for resizing

hot spot for resizing

Fig 2.6 The design form.

This form has all the usual features of a window. The hot spots are used for resizing the form. When the mouse pointer is on a hot spot a double ended arrow is shown. By pressing the left mouse button and dragging, the form border can be moved to shrink or enlarge the form. When the minimise button is pressed the form is reduced to an icon as shown in fig 2.7. Click on it to restore it.

Fig 2.7 Minimised forms.

The toolbox provides the tools to add **CommandButton**, **TextBox** and **Label** components, in fact all the other standard Windows elements that are your user interface. All of these elements are called "controls".

The grid dots are used to align controls. When you insert a control such as a **CommandButton** it will "snap" to the nearest grid point. You can alter the spacing of the grid points or disable the grid altogether. Each type of control has a set of configurable properties associated with it.

The Form Layout Window

The Form Layout window allows you to specify the position on a non-maximised form when the application runs as shown in fig 2.8.

You can move the form icon within the picture of the screen to the position that you want your form to appear when you run your application.

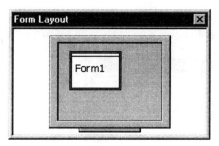

Fig 2.8 *The Form Layout window.*

The Project Explorer window

The Project Explorer window is significantly different to the project window found in earlier versions. It is shown in fig 2.9.

View Code icon →

View Object icon

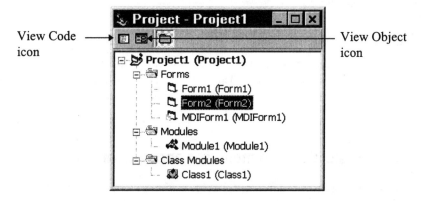

Fig 2.9 *The Project Explorer window.*

This gives a visual representation of the forms and modules in a project. If you select, for example, a form and then click on the View Code icon near the top of the window the code relating to the form will be displayed. Similarly by clicking on the View Object icon, the form itself is displayed.

The third icon toggles between a display where all the available forms and modules in the project are simply listed and one in which they are shown in a hierarchical tree structure as shown in fig 2.9.

The Properties window

The control Properties window lists all the properties of the form. When you add controls to the form a Properties window is created for each control, but only one

Properties window can be displayed at any time. **Caption** is one of the properties of a form which can be changed to give a more meaningful name than *Form1*.

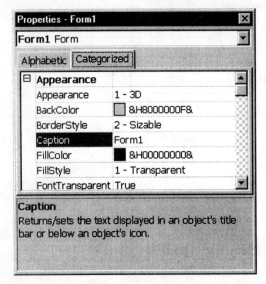

Fig 2.10 The Properties window.

A useful new feature in version 5 is that you can display the properties either alphabetical or grouped by category. This is helpful if you know the function of a property but are not sure of its name. Clicking on the page tab at the top of the window switches between these two types of display.

The Visual Basic standard menu bar and toolbar

The Visual Basic menu bar shown in fig 2.11 is directly under the title bar. Visual Basic 5 has four different menu bars. The one shown is the standard bar.

Fig 2.11 The standard menu bar.

This type of menu system is familiar to anyone who has used a Windows program. The options on the Visual Basic menu bar are:

- **File** allows you to open and save files and projects.
- **Edit** provides editing options such as **Cut** and **Paste** and **Search**.
- **View** determines what parts of the environment are displayed. If, for example, you lose the toolbox or project window the **View** menu will display it for you.
- **Project** allows you to add modules and forms to a project.

- **Format** provides a set of tools for arranging objects on forms.
- **Debug** gives a set of debug facilities, which allow you to step through your code and to use watchpoints.
- **Run** starts the program running, restarts it if it is paused during debugging, or stops it.
- **Tools** allows you to control key features about the project and run-time environment, such as the first form to be displayed when an application is run. It also provides a menu editor.
- **Add-ins** option runs the **Add-in Manager** and the **Property Page Wizard**.
- **Window** provides a set of options which determine the position and visibility of windows currently available
- **Help** option provides a comprehensive help facility.

The toolbar provides a shortcut way of invoking the most common features on the menu bar. All of these are looked at in detail later, but the best way to learn Visual Basic is to write an application

The toolbox

The toolbox is used to put the controls such as the **CommandButton**, and **TextBox** onto a form. The toolbox contains a number of controls which represent all the Windows objects that you can use when designing your application interface. The toolbox controls are shown in fig. 2.12.

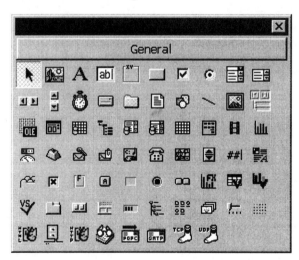 

Fig 2.12 The toolbox, with and without the custom controls.

The right figure shows a standard set of controls while the left figure contains a large number of custom controls which you can add. In addition to adding controls supplied with Visual Basic or by a third party vendor, Visual Basic allows you to write your own custom controls.

The controls are placed on the form by clicking on the control that you want in the toolbox. Press the left mouse button when the cursor is over the form in the position that you want the top left or bottom right of the control to appear on that form. Drag the mouse with the button still pressed. A box appears which defines the area of the control. When you release the button this position marks the opposite corner of the control which is displayed. Both the position and the size of the controls can be altered at any time. Most programmers would position the controls approximately and fine-tune later. Chapters 5 and 15 cover the standard and most common custom controls.

The best way to learn about programming in Visual Basic is to create an application and to see how the controls perform. We do this in the next chapter.

3

Shrinking and Growing

Introduction

The best way to learn a new programming language and its environment is to use it.
In this chapter you will learn about:

- Creating a new project.
- The **CommandButton** and **Image** controls.
- How to move and scale controls.
- How to save projects.

Outline of the Shrinking and Growing program

The *Shrinking and Growing* program displays a picture which you can alter the size of.

Fig 3.1 The Shrinking and Growing application at run-time.

When you click on the button with the caption *Bigger*, the picture increases in size. When you click on the button with the *Smaller* caption it decreases. The final user interface will be similar to the one shown in fig 3.1.

Creating a new project

The first stage in any program is to create a new project:

- Select the **File** menu.
- Select the **New Project** option as shown in fig 3.2.

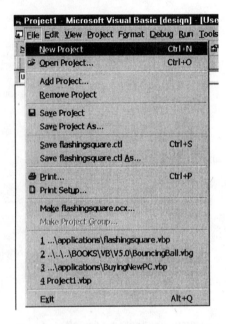

Fig 3.2 Creating a new project.

- If you have been experimenting with Visual Basic before trying this application you will be asked if you wish to save the existing project as shown in fig 3.3.
- If you do not want to keep it click on **No**.

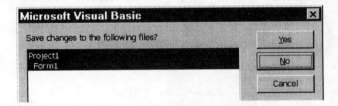

Fig 3.3 Saving an existing project.

If you have not created any application so far, you will not see this window.

- You will be prompted with the New Project window as shown in fig 3.4.
- Select the **Standard EXE** option.

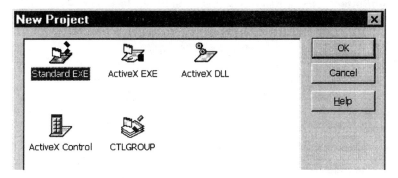

Fig 3.4 Choosing the project type.

Next you need to define the user interface and write the code to process the input data.

Defining the user interface

The window headed *Form1* is where you define your user interface. The window can be scaled or moved in the usual way for a window, by dragging on one of the handles. To add controls to the form you use the toolbox.

There are two ways of displaying the toolbox, either:

- Click on the toolbox iconon the menu bar as shown in fig 3.5.

Fig 3.5 The toolbox icon.

- Select The **View | Toolbox** menu option.

Fig 3.6 The standard toolbox.

The standard toolbox is shown in fig 3.6. Your toolbox may be in a differently sized window. You can resize the window in any way you wish using the sizing handles.

In this program we are going to use only two controls, the **Image** control and the **CommandButton**. They are shown in figs 3.7 and 3.8.

*Fig 3.7 The **Image** control.*

*Fig 3.8 The **CommandButton** control.*

To add the controls to the form:

- From the toolbox click on the **CommandButton** control.
- Position the cursor on the form roughly where you want the **CommandButton** to go.
- Press the left mouse button, and drag to give the size of button that you want.
- Select the **CommandButton** on the toolbox again.
- Place a second **CommandButton** control on the form.
- Select the **Image** control and place it on the form in the same way.

Moving and scaling

All the controls on a form can be moved about on the form. Each control can have its size changed, both horizontally and vertically.

Any component can be selected by clicking on it. A group of components can be selected by pressing the left mouse button and dragging.. As you do this a rectangle appears. All controls that are completely within the rectangle are selected.

Selected components can be moved by pressing the left mouse button on a selected area, not on one of the handles, and dragging.

All the control boxes and buttons created can be scaled by clicking on the corner or side handles of a selected control and dragging the handle. This can be done at any stage to enhance the appearance of your user interface.

If you want to delete a control, select it and press the **Delete** key.

The Properties window

When a control is created it has a set of default properties. When a control is selected its properties are automatically displayed in its Properties window. By selecting the Properties window the properties of the control can be viewed and modified.

There are three ways of displaying the Properties window, either:

- Click on the icon on the menu bar as shown in fig 3.9.
- Select the **View | Properties Window** menu option.
- Press **F4**.

Fig 3.9 Displaying the Properties window.

When you change any property of an object the properties shown in the Properties window are changed and are immediately reflected in the current application being developed.

- The object box is displayed just under the title bar. This displays the name of the object that currently holds the focus and what type of object it is.
- In fig 3.10 the object is called *Command1* and is of type **CommandButton**.
- At the bottom of the window is a description of the currently selected property.
- The settings column displays the value of the selected property and allows you to modify it.
- You can display the properties in alphabetical order or by category by selecting either the **Alphabetic** or **Categorized** pages. The default is **Alphabetic**.

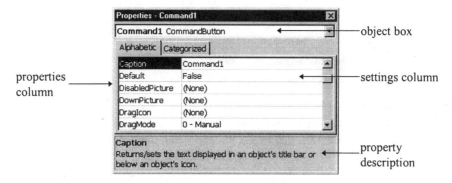

Fig 3.10 The Properties window.

Changing captions

You can select an object by clicking on it. When you select an object, that object is said to "have the focus". The properties of the selected object are displayed in the Properties window. If you want to change the property of an object, select it, find the property that you want to change, and select the settings column. The changes are immediately shown in the object. Some objects do not have a lot of properties and you will be able to see all of them displayed at the same time in the Properties window. If it is not possible to see them all in the window, you can scroll up and down the list, using the vertical scroll bar on the window.

The first property that we are going to change is the **Caption** property of the form:

- Select the form, by clicking on any part of the form that does not contain another object, (such as the button or image objects).
- This will cause the Properties window to display the properties of this control.
- Select the **Caption** property and change to *Shrinking and Growing* as shown in fig 3.11.

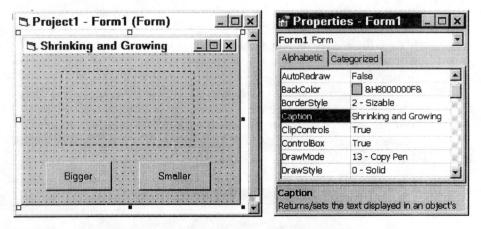

*Fig 3.11 Changing the **Caption** property of the form.*

Change the properties of the two buttons in a similar way:

- Select the buttons in turn.
- Change the **Caption** property of the left button to *Bigger.*
- Change the **Caption** property of the right button to *Smaller.*

Displaying a picture

To display a picture in the **Image** control we need to change the **Picture** property. This is a little more complicated than changing the **Caption** property:

- Select the **Image** object.
- Select the **Picture** property of this object.
- Click on the small button on the right side of this property. This displays the **Load Picture** window, which prompts you to choose the file containing the

image you wish to display as shown in fig 3.12. You can browse through your files using the standard controls on the toolbar of this window.

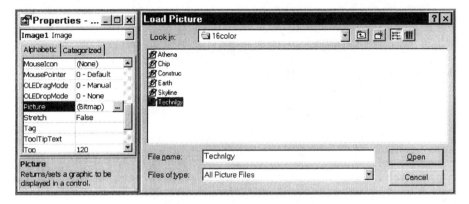

*Fig 3.12 Changing the **Picture** property of the **Image** object.*

The name of the image file is not displayed in the **Properties** window, but its type, bitmap in this case, is displayed.

The current form is shown in fig 3.13, although the picture in your application will be different.

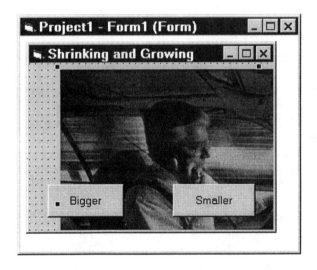

Fig 3.13 The application at design time.

One of the first things that you will notice is that the picture displayed is not the same size as the **Image** control you created (unless you were lucky in choosing a picture of exactly the right size!). If you do attempt to change the size of the picture by dragging on the sizing handles of the image, the size of the **Image** control will change, but the picture will remain unchanged.   The size of the **Image** control simply determines how much of the picture you will see and the amount of blank space around it. If you want to be able to resize the whole image, change the **Stretch** property from the default value of **False** to **True**.

Supported file types

Visual Basic supports a wide range of image file formats, including all of the standard ones you are likely to use:

Table 3.1 Supported file types.

File type	File extension
Bitmap.	BMP, DIB.
GIF.	GIF.
JPG.	JPG.
Metafile.	WMF, EMF.
Icon.	ICO.

If you want to display all the file types when browsing for your picture, choose the **All Picture Files** option from the **Files of type** list as shown in fig 3.12.

Common problems

When you are learning a new language and development environment and trying to follow a sequence of detailed instructions, things can go wrong. One of the most common mistakes is to change the **Name** property of the form rather than the **Caption** property. It is easy to do this since the default name of the first form is *Form1*, this is also the default value of the **Caption** property. The **Caption** property is the title which is displayed on the title bar of the form. The **Name** property is how this object is referred to by other objects in the application. This was recognised as a problem in version 4 and so in a half hearted attempt to address the problem, the **Name** property is always at the top of the alphabetic listing in the **Properties** window and is in brackets to make it stand out.

If you do accidentally change the **Name** property rather than the **Caption** property, the title bar of the form will not be changed. To correct this select the **Name** property and change it back to *Form1*, then make the necessary changes to the **Caption** property.

Another common problem occurs when adding the picture. Forms and many other types of objects also have a **Picture** property and it is easy to accidentally select the form rather than the **Image** control.

Running the program

You have now created an application which you can run, although the two buttons will not do anything yet. The completed *Shrinking and Growing* application at design time is shown in fig 3.14.

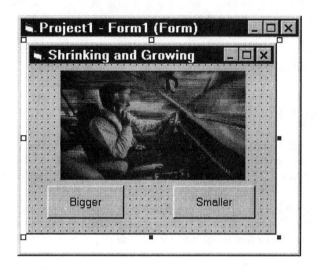

Fig 3.14 *The completed Shrinking and Growing application at design time.*

There are two ways to run the application either:

- Press the **Run** button on the toolbar as shown in fig 3.15.
- Select the **Run | Start** menu option.

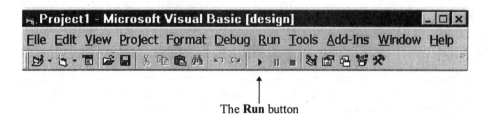

The **Run** button

Fig 3.15 *Running the completed program.*

The application is not complete yet, but it already does quite a lot. When it is run, the buttons and the picture are displayed. You can maximise and minimise the form and move it around the screen. You can resize the form. You can end the application by clicking on the finish button in the top right corner.

If you just wanted to develop a prototype to see what the final version would look like, perhaps to show to a user or your manager, and to get feedback on the user interface, Visual Basic 5 is an ideal tool. You do not have to have a fully working application to give a feel of what the finished product will be like. An increasingly popular way of developing software is to create a prototype to help you see what the final application may look like and to modify your design if you see aspects which could be improved. Some purists still feel that the user should specify what exactly what he wants and the software developer should then produce an application to this specification and present it to the user when it is complete. This idealist method is increasingly not used. Often users are not completely sure of what they want and seeing a prototype helps them to firm up their ideas. This is likely to mean that the design will need to be changed. Visual Basic is an ideal environment for this type of rapid prototyping.

Event driven software

If you have programmed before in languages such as Pascal or C in a DOS environment, you need to think in a different way to program in Visual Basic for Windows 95. When a Windows program runs, you are usually presented with a screen comprising a form with a number of controls. You decide what happens next by perhaps clicking on a button, selecting a list item or inputting text. Everything you do is viewed by the application as an event, and the programmer who wrote the application needs to make sure that every event that occurs is dealt with. This is called event driven software.

In Visual Basic every event has a name and an event procedure associated with it which makes a response to that event. If, for example, you double click on a **CommandButton** you need to write some Basic code to take some appropriate action. Visual Basic produces template event procedures for events which you want to respond to, you have to write some BASIC code which supplies the detail.

Making the buttons work

In order to make the two buttons functional you need to write some code. In a Windows program, applications are event driven. Every object has a set of events associated with it. When these events occur an event procedure is executed. If you want your application to take some action when an event, such as a button click occurs you need to add some code to the event procedure for that object. To write this code you need to view the Code window for the object, there are several to do this:

- Select the object, in this case the left button.
- Click the right mouse button to display the speed menu as shown in fig 3.16.

Fig 3.16 *The Code window.*

- Select the **View Code** option.

Alternatively:

- Select the object.
- Select the **View | Code** menu option.

The quickest way is to:

- Select the object.
- Double click on the object.

The code window for the **Click** event for the button called *Command1* is shown in fig 3.17. When you click on a button this causes a **Click** event. Visual Basic automatically creates the header and terminator for the procedure which processes the button click event as shown in fig 3.17.

event procedure template   object list   title bar   event list

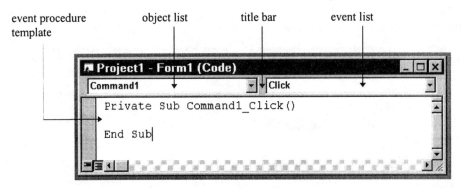

Fig 3.17 *The code window.*

You need to add some code to the **Click** event handler for the two buttons, so that one makes the image bigger when it is clicked and the other makes it smaller.

The template for the event procedure is shown below. This is created automatically by Visual Basic.

Private Sub *Command1_Click ( )*

End Sub

The procedure name consists of the control name, an underscore and the word *Click*. When an event occurs the program will execute the event procedure associated with this event.

There are two properties which control the dimensions of the **Image** control, **Height** and **Width**. To increase the value of these properties, you need to add the following two lines in between the two existing lines of the event procedure for the button which is going to make the image bigger:

*Image1.**Height** = Image1.**Height** + 10*
*Image1.**Width** = Image1.**Width** + 10*

- Since more than one object may have a **Height** or **Width** property, you need to state explicitly which object you are referring to. *Image1*.**Height** refers to the **Height** property of the object called *Image1*. Note that an object is identified by its **Name** property, not its **Caption** property.
- The **Height** and **Width** properties have 10 units added to their existing size by these two lines.
- You can change the default units that Visual Basic uses. This is covered in chapter 16.

In order to change the event procedure for the button which makes the image smaller, you can repeat one of the procedures used to find this event procedure. An alternative way is to click on the down arrow on the object list as shown in fig 3.18, and then select the second button, called *Command2*.

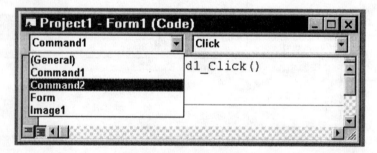

Fig 3.18 The code window.

If you wish to view the code for another event procedure click on the list of events and choose the one you want. You should choose the object first, since the list of available events is not the same for different classes of objects.

Similarly the event procedure for the button which makes the image smaller includes the lines:

$$Image1.\textbf{Height} = Image1.\textbf{Height} - 10$$
$$Image1.\textbf{Width} = Image1.\textbf{Width} - 10$$

When you have made these changes, the application will be fully functional. You should run it to make sure that it works correctly.

Applications in Visual Basic consist of a set of files organised into a project. Visual Basic does virtually all the management of files in a project for you. If you want to keep the application you have just created you need to save the project.

Saving the project

Before you save a project you should create a new folder. It is good practice to save each project in a different folder, since if you are using the default file names, the second project you save in a folder will overwrite the first.

The project can be saved by choosing the **File | Save Project** option as shown in fig 3.19. You will initially be prompted for the name and location of each component of the project, such as the forms. Finally the project file will be saved which contains details of the location of all parts of the project. This menu also gives you the option of creating a new folder.

move up one level _____| |_____ create a new folder

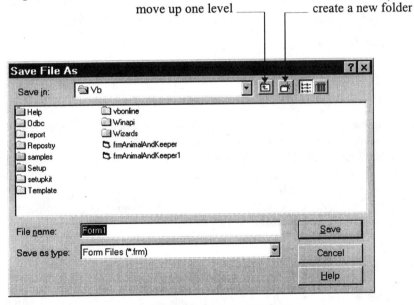

Fig 3.19 Saving a project.

The project file has an extension of VBP (Visual Basic Project). The next time you save a project you will not be prompted for a folder. If you wish to save your application in a different folder, choose the **File | Save Project As** menu option.

4
Managing Projects and Files

Introduction

The files which make up an application in Visual Basic are grouped together in a project. The first stage in developing an application is to create a new project, Visual Basic gives a default set of files which will be sufficient for simple applications. If you wish to add additional modules such as forms, it is straightforward to do so.

In this chapter you will learn about:

- The files in a Visual Basic project.
- Managing the files in a project.
- Adding and deleting project files.

It is essential when you add an element to your project or delete one, such as a form, that you use the facilities provided by the **File** and **Project** menus, rather than copying files using the Windows Explorer. Similarly, when you want to save a project in another folder or onto another disk you should use options on these menus rather than simply copying the files. Each project has a resource file which keeps a record of where every file in the project is stored. If you copy one or more files to another folder or disk, the resource file will be unable to find them.

Opening and closing projects

It is a good idea to create a new folder for every application that you write. If you rely on the default names that Visual Basic suggests for the files in your project you will find that existing files will be overwritten unless you use a new folder.

When you run Visual Basic you will be prompted either to open an existing project or to create a new one as shown in fig 4.1.

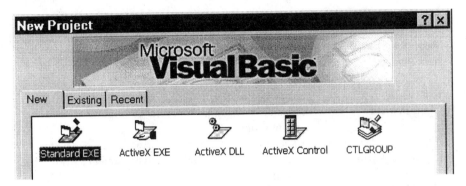

Fig 4.1 Creating a new project or opening an existing one.

Visual Basic 5, unlike earlier versions, allows you to have more than one project open at a time, although only one project may be active.

When you create a new project you will be prompted to specify which type of project you want to create. There are five possible options:

- **ActiveX control.**
- **ActiveX DLL.**
- **ActiveX EXE.**
- **Standard EXE.**
- **CTRLGROUP.**

Most of the applications you create will be standard Windows 95 executable.

If you are already running Visual Basic and you want to create a new project, choose **File | New Project** menu option, which is shown in fig 4.2.

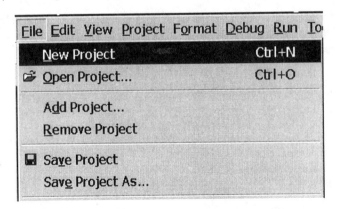

*Fig 4.2 The **File** menu.*

The **File** menu is critical to project management, the key options are listed in table 4.1.

Table 4.1 *Managing projects.*

Menu Command	Description
New Project	Starts a new project after prompting the user to save the current project. When you run Visual Basic a new project is automatically started.
Open Project	Loads an existing project after prompting to save the current project.
Add Project	Adds another project to the currently active desktop.
Remove Project	Removes the currently active project from the desktop.
Save Project	Saves all files associated with the current project.
Save Project As	Saves all existing project files and prompts the user for a project name.

When a project is being saved for the first time, you will be prompted for the name of each file in the project. The project (VBP) file is saved last, since this contains the location of all the project files. Manual modification of this file is not recommended. When you close an existing project it is saved in the same files and folders unless you choose the **Save Project As** option.

Every time that you start a new project it is advisable to use a new folder. If you have more than one project in a folder and rely on using the default names for the files in the project you will overwrite existing files.

Application files

The different aspects of a project are described in a collection of files. These files are used to build the application.

Projects consist of the following:

- One file for each form (FRM).
- One file for each code module (BAS).
- One file for each custom component (OCX).
- One project file which keeps a track of all the other components (VBP).
- One file per form is required to store an associated binary data item (FRX).
- A resource file (RES).
- User-defined control (CTL).
- A class file (CLS) for each class module.

The files in the project are combined to form a single executable Windows application (EXE).

The Project Explorer as shown in fig 4.3 shows all the files in the project. When you have saved the files in a project the names of the files are shown next in the Project Explorer.

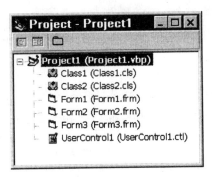

Fig 4.3 *The Project Explorer.*

You can display the Project Explorer by choosing that option from the **View** menu.

FRM files

Forms have an FRM extension. They contain:

- A full graphical description of the form.
- The controls on the form.
- The event procedures.
- Sometimes general procedures, although these are more usually contained in a BAS file.

Applications can have multiple forms, but each form is saved as a separate file.

BAS files

These files have changed their name in the last three versions of Visual Basic. They are called:

- Code modules in version 3.
- Standard modules in version 4.
- Modules in version 5.

Some of the Visual Basic documentation has not fully caught up with these changes, so you do need to be aware of them. The extension of BAS has remained unchanged. BAS files are modules that contain:

- Code independent of any form.
- General procedures not event driven procedures.
- Global and module declarations of types, constants and variables.

To create a new BAS file use the **Project | Add Module** menu option.
To add an existing module of any type use the **Project | Add File** menu option.

OCX files

Custom controls are built in Visual Basic and have an OCX extension. They include:

- The **Grid** control.
- The **CommonDialog** control.
- The **OLE** (Object Linking and Embedding) control.

Many third parties are selling a wide range of OCX files or VBX files, which are 16-bit versions of the 32-bit OCX controls. OCX and VBX files are installed in the Windows System directory. If you want to see the custom controls that you have installed - or wish to install another, choose the **Project | Components** menu option as shown in fig 4.4.

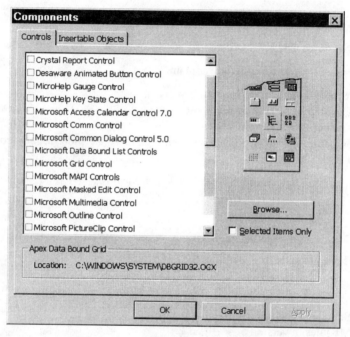

*Fig 4.4 The **CommonDialog** controls.*

The OCX files can also be user-defined ActiveX controls. They are similar to the VBX files except that VBX files can only be used with 16 bit versions of Visual Basic, while OCX files can be used in both 16 and 32 bit applications. It is advisable to replace your VBX controls from earlier versions of Visual Basic with OCX files.

FRX files

FRX files are used for storing binary data.

- Some controls, such as the **PictureBox** control have a **Picture** property for displaying an image. The binary picture is stored in an FRX file.
- One FRX file at most per form.
- FRX files are managed by Visual Basic without user intervention.
- FRX files have the same name as the associated form.

CTL files

When you create a control in Visual Basic you are creating a control class, that is a description of a class which is used to create controls. When you add a user created control to an application you are adding an instance of the control class. The CTL file contains a description of the control class.

CLS files

A class or CLS module is used to define a class, that is the code which defines the properties and methods of the class, as well as the properties that determine the behaviour of a class. Object oriented class programming and the roles of classes and objects is discussed later in chapter 12.

To create a new class file choose **Project | Add Class Module** menu option.

Adding elements to a project

The **Project** menu is used for adding forms, modules and other objects to a project. The key entries for the **Project** menu are listed in table 4.2.

*Table 4.2 The **Project** menu.*

Menu Command	Description
Add Form	When you create a new project Visual Basic gives you one form as a default. If you want to add other forms to your project choose this option.
Add MDI Form	Adds a Multiple Document Interface (MDI) form to the project. This is discussed in chapter 6.
Add Module	Adds a module, that is a BAS file, to the project.
Add Class Module	A class module has an extension of CLS. Class modules define the properties and methods of a class. This option allows you to add an existing class module or to create a new one. Class modules are described in chapter 12.
Add User Control	Controls have an extension of CTL. This option allows you to add an existing control or to create a new one.

When a project is being saved, the project (VBP) file is saved last, since this contains the location of all the project files. Modification of this file is not recommended.

A common problem

If you add or remove a file from a project, the project file is updated. If a file is deleted outside of Visual Basic, this may cause problems as the project file will be incorrect. It makes sense to deal with all changes to the files in a project by using the Visual Basic menu system.

A common difficulty occurs when you want to save your project on a floppy or in a new folder. If you use the Windows Explorer to copy files, the application may not run, since the project file which lists the location of all the files in the project will still be pointing to the locations on the original file system. You need to use the **File | Save Project As** menu option to save your project in another location.

It is important to note that if an existing file is added to a project, a copy of it is not made - there is simply a reference to it in the project file, so any file, form or module can be a part of more than one project.

5

Standard Controls

Introduction

We have already looked at a few of the standard controls, this chapter gives you all the essential information that you need on the most commonly used standard controls to develop major applications. All controls have a set of properties and methods which operate on them.

In this chapter you will learn about:

- The toolbox.
- The standard controls.
- Essential methods and properties of the standard controls.

All the controls covered in this section are those available in all versions of Visual Basic.

The toolbox appearance

If you cannot find the toolbox click on the toolbox icon, shown in fig 5.1 or select the **View | Toolbox** option from the menu.

                    Fig 5.1 *The toolbox icon.*

Your toolbox will probably look like the one shown below on the right of fig 5.2. This toolbox shows only the standard controls. At the other extreme if you have added custom controls or created your own it may look more like the one on the left. Chapter 15 covers the use of the most popular custom controls.

In this chapter we are going to look at the controls in the standard toolbox.

Fig 5.2 The toolbox with and without some custom controls.

Adding controls to forms

If you want to add a control to a form:

- Select the control by clicking on it. A border will appear around the control.
- Click on the form in the position that you want either the top left or the bottom right of the control to appear.
- As the mouse is dragged, the size and position of the control is seen.

After doing this you will notice that the control you selected on the toolbox is now de-selected. If you want to add another control of the same type you can repeat the above procedure, or use a slightly different technique:

- Press the **Ctrl** button.
- Keeping the **Ctrl** button pressed select the control you want on the toolbox.
- Click on the form and drag to add the control as before.
- Click on the second position and drag to add subsequent controls.

When you have added all the controls of this type that you want, click on another icon on the toolbox.

Selecting controls

The easiest way to see the properties of a control is to select it. The properties are shown in the Properties window. Select a control by clicking on it. Eight sizing handles are displayed on a selected control.

There are two ways to select more than one control at the same time:

- Click on the form and drag the mouse. A rectangle is produced which will select all of the controls which are fully or partially controlled with it. If you have a simple form, this is often the best way to select a group of controls, however it is not always possible to include only the required controls by this method.

- The alternative is to click on the required controls whilst holding the **Shift** key.

Cutting and Pasting

You can cut and paste controls using the edit facilities on the **Edit** menu or the edit toolbar. You can transfer controls or groups of controls between forms or applications using cut and paste. If you do copy a control it will have exactly the same properties as the original control, including the **Name** property. If you try to paste it to a form which already has a control of that name this will clearly cause a problem, since Visual Basic must be able to distinguish between controls. If you attempt to have more than one control with the same name on a form, the warning message shown in fig 5.3 is shown.

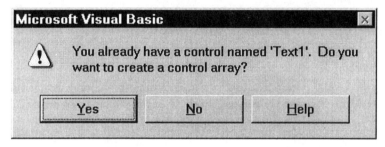

Fig 5.3 Warning message when copying controls.

If you select **No**, the control you are pasting will be given the next default name - in this case *Text2*, if *Text1* is the only existing text box.

If you select **Yes,** a control arrays is created. These are covered in detail in chapter 12.

Common toolbox controls

     Pointer. This does not draw a control, but is used to select an existing control.

     PictureBox. This control displays graphical images and acts as a container for graphics methods.

Label. Holds text that does not change.

 TextBox. Holds text that you can enter and change.

 Frame. Groups controls together, such as **OptionButtons**.

 CommandButton. A button that can be clicked at run-time.

 CheckBox. A **True/False** box.

 OptionButton. It is used with other options buttons to display a range of choices, only one of which may be selected.

 ComboBox. A combined **ListBox** and **TextBox**. An item from the list can be selected or text entered.

 ListBox. You can select one entry from a displayed list.

 HScrollBar and **VScrollBar**. Horizontal and vertical scroll bars. Used as tools for scrolling through a lot of information, or as an input control.

 Timer. Used to trap timer events at specified intervals.

 DriveListBox. Used to display available drives.

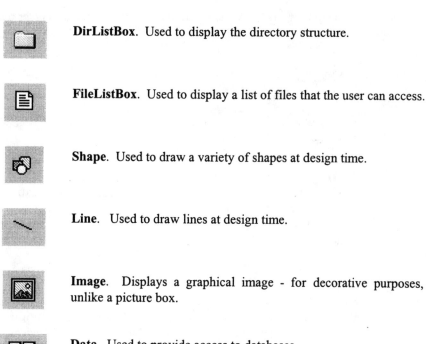

DirListBox. Used to display the directory structure.

FileListBox. Used to display a list of files that the user can access.

Shape. Used to draw a variety of shapes at design time.

Line. Used to draw lines at design time.

Image. Displays a graphical image - for decorative purposes, unlike a picture box.

Data. Used to provide access to databases.

OLE. Provides Object Linking and Embedding from an OLE server into your application.

The pointer icon

The pointer icon is not a control, but when it is active, (that is when it has the focus) you can select any control or group of controls on a form. Only one control (or the pointer icon) on the toolbox can have the focus at any time.

Common properties

There are some properties that most controls have in common:

- **Name**. How Visual Basic identifies the control.
- **Top** and **Left**. The position of the control relative to the form.
- **Height** and **Width**. The size of the control.
- **Visible**. If this property is **True** the control can be seen.
- **Enabled**. If set to **False** the user cannot access this control at run-time.

- **ToolTipText**. This text is displayed at run-time when the cursor moves over the control as shown in fig 5.4.

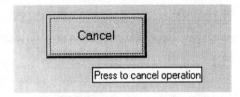

*Fig 5.4 The **ToolTipText** property.*

- **TabIndex**. When more than one control is displayed on a form you can move between the controls in rotation by pressing the **Tab** key.   The **TabIndex** determines the order in which the application moves between the controls.   Default values are assigned at design-time, but these can be changed.

The PictureBox control

If you want to add a picture to your application the **PictureBox** control can act as a container. When you first add a **PictureBox** control to a form the **Picture** property will be set to **(None)**. To add a picture select the **Picture** property in the Property window and click on the button with three dots on the right of this property as shown in fig 5.5. You will be shown a window which will allow you to browse and find the image you want.

*Fig 5.5 Displaying images using the **PictureBox** control.*

If the **AutoSize** property is set to **True** the control will automatically resize so that it fits the image exactly. The **PictureBox** control is discussed in more detail in chapter 16 which looks at using graphics in your applications.

The Label control

Label controls can be used to display a small amount of text. **Labels** are usually placed alongside a **TextBox** to prompt the user for the information that he is expected to enter into the **TextBox**:

- The **Caption** property contains the text which is displayed.
- If the **AutoSize** property is **True**, the label changes its horizontal size to fit the text.
- If the **WordWrap** property is **True**, the label changes its vertical size to fit the text.
- Text can be left justified, right justified or centred using the **Alignment** property.
- The first label is called *Label1* the second *Label2* and so on.

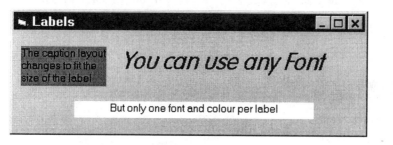

*Fig 5.6 Creating a **Label** control.*

An important limitation of the label is that while you have full control over the colour, font and text size of a label, you can only have one colour and font in a label.

The TextBox Control

The **TextBox** control is probably the most commonly used control, since it is used for either displaying or entering a lot of text.

- The contents of the **TextBox** are determined by the **Text** property.
- You can control the maximum amount of text that the text box can display by setting the **MaxLength** property to the maximum number of characters. The default is 0, which means that there is no limit. When you are typing more than one line of text lines are ended by typing **Ctrl+Return**.
- The **MultiLine** property allows you to have more than one line of text.
- You can add scroll bars by setting the **ScrollBars** property of the **TextBox** to horizontal, vertical or both. This property is not active unless the **MultiLine** property is **True**.

A few examples are shown in fig 5.7.

Fig 5.7 Typical text boxes.

- The **BorderStyle** property alters the appearance of the **TextBox** as shown in fig 5.8.
- The format of the **TextBox** can also be controlled by the **ScrollBars** properties.

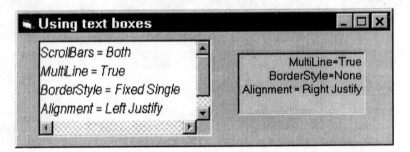

*Fig 5.8 The **BorderStyle** and **ScrollBars** property.*

Passwords

A useful feature of the **TextBox** control is that it can be used to input passwords.

- The designer can set the **PasswordChar** property to any character, for example, "*".
- When you type text into this box, each key depression is reflected by this character being displayed in the text box.
- The **MaxLength** property can be used to limit the number of characters in the password.
- The actual text typed is available for your program to use.

Captions and hot keys

Captions are used to identify controls. You can use the default captions or choose your own. You can also use the **Captions** property to create "hot keys".

- For example, if you have a button with a caption of **Quit** and you want **Alt+Q** to be equivalent to pressing this button, set the caption to **&Quit**.
- The "&" character means that **Alt** in conjunction with the following letter can be used to invoke this command.

The Frame control

The **Frame** control is used to group together sets of controls.

- The **Caption** property controls the text at the top of the frame.
- **OptionButton** controls placed on a **Frame** behave as a group, that is only one **OptionButton** on a frame may be checked as shown in fig 5.9. The **Frame** shown contains a **PictureBox** control in addition to the **OptionButtons**.
- Controls placed on a **Frame** can be moved as a single group.

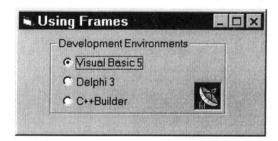

*Fig 5.9 The **Frame** control.*

Controls cannot be grouped by placing a frame around them. The **Frame** must be created first and new controls added to it.

The CommandButton control

One of the most common controls you will use is the **CommandButton**. Some typical command buttons are shown in fig 5.10:

- The value of the **Caption** property and the **Name** property of the first button is *Command1*, the second *Command2* and so on.
- Normally when you press the **Escape** key, no action is taken, that is the previous action is cancelled, this is usually equivalent to pressing a **Cancel** button. If you want to make a button the **Cancel** button for a form, then you

should assign its **Cancel** property to **True**. The action taken on pressing **Escape** will be the same as giving the **Cancel** button the focus and pressing **Return**. Only one button on a form can have its **Cancel** property set to **True**, the others are automatically set to **False**.

- If you want your button to contain a picture set the **Style** property to **True**. You can add three different pictures to a button. The **Picture** property assigns a default picture. The **DownPicture** property is the picture displayed when the button is pressed and the **DisabledPicture** property is the picture displayed when the **Enabled** property of the button is **False**.
- The key event associated with the button is the **Click** event.

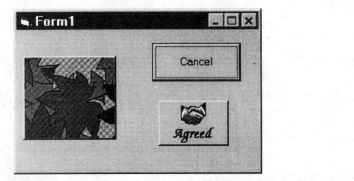

Fig 5.10 Varieties of CommandButtons.

The CheckBox control

The **CheckBox** and **OptionButton** controls are similar in that they allow the user to specify a **True/False** or **Yes/No** answer. The key difference apart from minor differences in appearance is that only one **OptionButton** in a container can be **True**. This is not the case for **CheckBox** controls. **CheckBox** controls are often displayed in a frame as shown in fig 5.11 to show that they are logically grouped together.

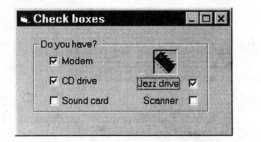

Fig 5.11 The CheckBox control.

- The **Caption** property determines the text displayed alongside the box.

- The **Alignment** property can be **Left Justify** or **Right Justify**, this determines if the text is on the right or left of the checkable square.
- **CheckBox** controls have a **Value** property, which can have three possible settings:

Table 5.1 *The Value property for CheckBox control.*

Value	Description
0	The **CheckBox** is deselected.
1	The **CheckBox** is selected.
2	The **CheckBox** is not available to the user.

The OptionButtons control

This control is very similar to the **CheckBox** control:

- **OptionButton** controls always appear in groups and only one of the group can be selected at a time.
- If you place more than one **OptionButton** directly onto a form rather than onto a **Frame** control you will only be able to set one of them.
- The **Caption** property determines the text placed alongside the button.
- The **Alignment** property determines if the text is on the right or left.
- The **Value** property which determines the state of the button behaves in the same way as for **CheckBox** controls.

An example of several **OptionButton** controls on a **Frame** is shown in fig 5.9.

The ComboBox control

The **ComboBox** control is shown in fig 5.12.

Fig 5.12 *The ComboBox control.*

The **ComboBox** control combines the features of a **TextBox** and a **ListBox** control. It is one of the most complex to use, it is in fact three different types of control. The type that a particular control represents is determined by the **Style** property, which can be assigned to one of the three styles shown in table 5.2.

Table 5.2 The Style property of the ComboBox control.

Type of ComboBox	Description
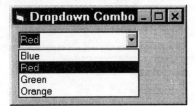	Dropdown combo; A combined **ListBox** and **TextBox** controls. You can select one of the options in the list or type a new entry.
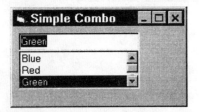	Simple combo; A **TextBox** and a **ListBox** which does not drop down. You can either select from the list or type. The **Height** property determines how many of the list items are displayed.
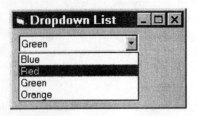	Dropdown list; You may only select one of the options provided in the list.

The ListBox control

A **ListBox** control allow you to select items from a list. It acts like a small window which shows a few of the possible options available and allows the user to scroll the list. An example is shown in fig 5.13.

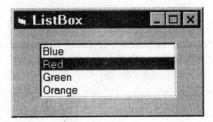

Fig 5.13 The ListBox control.

ListBox and **ComboBox** controls are very similar in appearance but differ in their operation. In a **ListBox** the items are fixed by the program, for example, a list of files in a directory. The user can select an item by using the arrowed keys to move to the appropriate item. The user can also search by typing in characters. The cursor is moved to the next item that has this character first. If necessary, the search wraps from the end of the list to the beginning.

Individual items in a **ListBox** can be referenced by using a subscript and the **List** property, for example the fourth entry in a **ListBox** called *MyList* is *MyList*.**List**(3). The first entry is *MyList*.**List**(0).

The AddItem method

Items can be added to a list in a **ListBox** or a **ComboBox** control using the **AddItem** method. The syntax of **AddItem** is:

> *[form.] control.**AddItem** item[, index]*

- *item* is the item to be added to the list.
- *index* is the index where the item is to be added. The default is to add the item to the end of the list. The list index starts from zero.

For example:

> *Country.**AddItem** "Germany"*
> *Country.**AddItem** "USA"*
> *Country.**AddItem** "France"*
> *Country.**AddItem** "Italy"*

The program statements used to put items in a list are usually put into the procedure which loads the form containing the list.

The Sorted property

The **ListBox** has a property called **Sorted**. If this is set to **True**, the items in the list are alphabetically sorted at run-time; otherwise they appear in the order in which they were added to the list.

The use of the *index* field may interfere with the sort mechanism. The syntax of setting the **Sorted** property is:

> *[form.]{ComboBox | ListBox}.**Sorted***

When the user clicks on a **ListBox** a selection can be made by scrolling through the list. The size of the list box is not expanded during the selection process.

The HScrollBar and VScrollBar controls

Scroll bars are a useful form of user interface, for example, in word processors for moving through the document. There are two forms - vertical and horizontal:

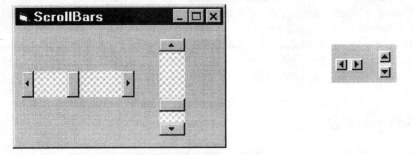

Fig 5.14 Scroll bars.

- The minimum value in a scroll bar is at the left/top.
- The maximum value in a scroll bar is at the right/bottom.
- The **Value** property gives an indication of how far the bar is moved between its maximum and minimum.
- The **Min** property gives the minimum value. The default is 0.
- The **Max** property gives the maximum value. The default is 32767.

The Timer control

When this control has its **Enabled** property set to **True** it will count down from the value specified in the **Interval** property (in milliseconds) to zero. When this interval has expired a **Timer** event occurs. Unless the **Enabled** property is set to **False** another **Timer** event will occur after **Interval** milliseconds.

*Fig 5.15 The **Timer** control.*

- There is no practical limit to the number of timers you can use.
- At design time a timer is of fixed size.
- At run-time a timer is invisible.
- A user cannot access a **Timer** control.
- The **Interval** property is in milliseconds with a maximum value of 65,535.

The Shape, Line and Image Controls

If you want to develop applications that not only work well but also look good to users you will often want to use graphics. In addition to the **PictureBox** control covered earlier in this chapter, the **Image**, **Shape** and **Line** controls can be used to add pictures. This is an important area and is covered in detail in chapter 16.

6

Buying a New PC

Introduction

The best way to learn how to use the controls and properties that we have looked at so far is to develop an application to see how they behave in practice. We are going to do this next. The aim is not to develop all the underlying code, but to develop an excellent user interface and to use a wide range of controls.

Forms are the containers for most Visual Basic applications, and this chapter looks at the behaviour of these vitally important objects.

In this chapter you will learn about:

- Designing a substantial form.
- Using controls.
- MDI and SDI forms.
- Modal and non-modal forms.
- Hiding and showing forms.

Design of the form

The application we are going to look at is the type of form that might be used when ordering a new PC. Most of the controls that you have seen so far are included on the form. The completed, running application is shown in fig 6.1.

To start developing this application you should do the following:

- Start a new project.
- Change the **Caption** property of the form to *Buying a new PC*.
- Add a **PictureBox** control in the bottom corner and change the **Picture** property so that a graphic is displayed which represents the company logo.
- Add a **Label** below the **PictureBox** and change its caption to *Mega Systems*.

- Change the **Font** property to a more interesting one than the standard San Serif font. The one used in fig 6.1 is 12 point italic *ZurichCalligraphic* font.

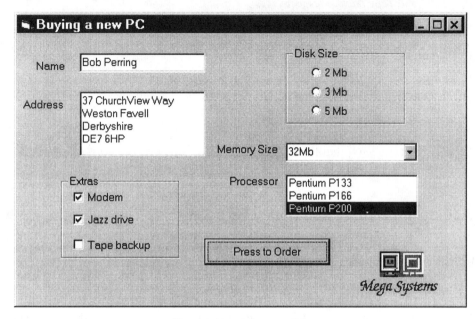

Fig 6.1 Buying a new PC.

Adding the TextBox controls

The name and address are entered in two **TextBox** controls:

- Add the first **TextBox** to represent the name.
- Change the **Caption** property so that it is blank, otherwise it will display the default text of *Text1*.
- Add the second **TextBox** to represent the address.
- Change the **MultiLine** property to **True**, since addresses will need more than one line.
- Change the **Text** property to be blank.
- Add **Label** controls adjacent to the **TextBox** controls, changing their captions to *Name* and *Address*.

Adding the CheckBox controls

The **CheckBox** controls are placed within a frame. This has no effect on the way they behave in the final application, but it does visually group them together:

- Add a **Frame** control to the form.

- Change the **Caption** property to *Extras*.
- Add three **CheckBox** controls changing their captions to *Modem*, *Jazz drive*, and *Tape backup* respectively.

Adding the OptionButton Controls

The **OptionButton** controls are also within a **Frame**, but this does have an important effect. Only one of these **OptionButtons** can be checked at any time:

- Add a **Frame** to the form.
- Change the **Caption** to *Disk Size*.
- Add three **OptionButton** controls, changing their captions to *2 Mb*, *3 Mb* and *5 Mb*, respectively.

Adding the ListBox and ComboBox controls

The memory size is specified using a **ComboBox** control, whilst the processor is specified using a **ListBox** control:

- Add the **ComboBox** control to the form.
- Change the **Style** property to **Dropdown Combo.**
- This control will allow you to choose one of the options available or to type your own text.
- The options in the **ComboBox** controls are specified at run-time by writing some code.
- Add a **ListBox** control, making it sufficiently large to display three listed items.
- The options for **ListBox** controls must also be specified at run-time.
- Add **Label** controls along side the **ComboBox** and **ListBox** controls and change their captions to *Memory Size* and *Processor*.
- Finally add a button to the form and change its caption to *Press to Order*.

If you are not satisfied with the appearance of the form, you can move or resize controls. If you want to remove a control, select it and press **Delete**.

Running the program

The form is beginning to resemble the finished result. The program can be run by selecting the **Run | Start** menu option or by pressing **F5** or by pressing the **Run** icon on the menu bar.

Note the following points:

- Only one of the **OptionButton** controls can be set at a time.
- Any number of **CheckBox** controls can be set.

- Text cannot be typed into the **ComboBox**.
- Text can be typed into the **TextBox** controls.
- Text can be selected.
- The **ListBox** and **ComboBox** are empty.

Initialising the ListBox and ComboBox

The **ComboBox** and **ListBox** controls need to be initialised. This can only be done at run-time. The best time is when the form is loaded in the *Form_Load* event.

Double click on the form to go to the code associated with form loading and add the following code:

```
Private Sub Form_Load ()
    Combo1.AddItem "16Mb"
    Combo1.AddItem "32Mb"
    Combo1.AddItem "64Mb"
    List1.AddItem "Pentium P133"
    List1.AddItem "Pentium P166"
    List1.AddItem "Pentium P200"
End Sub
```

The **AddItem** method is used to load up the combo and list box choices at run-time. When the program is run, you can select an item from the **ListBox** and the **ComboBox**, however the **ComboBox** still has *Combo1*, its default text, displayed as shown in fig 6.2.

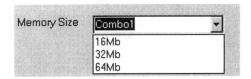

*Fig 6.2 Initialising the **ComboBox**.*

To display one of the list items as a default, add the following line of code to the form load event handler:

*Combo1.**ListIndex** = 1*

This will make *32 Mb* the default entry. *16 Mb* is the first item in the **ComboBox** and has a **ListIndex** property value of 0.

If you want a blank space displayed in place of a particular list item, assign **ListIndex** the value of -1.

You can also assign the **ListBox** a default value, for example, by the statement:

*List1.**ListIndex** = 2*

When you have selected an item in a **ComboBox** or **ListBox** control the value of the item you have selected is stored in the **Index** property. If no item is stored this value is -1;

TabIndex and TabStop

At run-time you can move between controls by pressing the **Tab** button.

- The order is controlled by the **TabIndex** property of the controls.
- The control with the **TabIndex** value of 0 is read first and so on.
- If you change one of the **TabIndex** values all the other **TabIndex** values for the other controls are automatically adjusted.
- If you want a control to be skipped, you can set the value of its **TabStop** property to **False**.

If you have made all of these changes you will now have a fully functioning user interface. Chapters 7, 8 and 9 will show you how to write the background code needed to make the application function fully.

Forms

Forms are more than just containers for holding controls, they have their own properties and methods, which it is important to understand in order to write applications that behave exactly how you want them to behave. The next section looks at forms and their properties, and how to use them to your advantage.

Controlling form properties

Most of the time you can use the default properties of the form, however Visual Basic does offer great flexibility in the way in which you can control every aspect of the form.

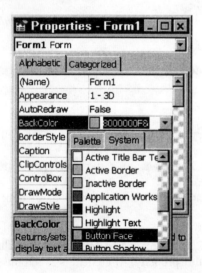 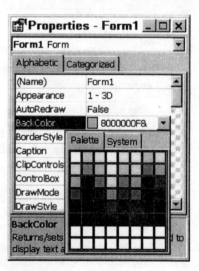

*Fig 6.3 The **BackColor** property.*

- One of the most commonly changed properties of a form is the background colour of the form. In order to see the colours available, select the **BackColor** property this property and click on down arrow in fig 6.3.
- You can choose a colour from either the **System** page, which lists the colour of components of your Windows system or the **Palette** page which allows you to choose any colour.

The **BorderStyle** property has six possible settings as shown in table 6.1.

*Table 6.1 The **BorderStyle** property.*

Property Value	Effect
vbBSNone	The form has no border.
vbFixedSingle	A fixed single border, resizable only using the maximise and minimise buttons.
vbSizable	The default. The border has minimise and maximise buttons. It is resizable.
vbFixedDouble	A fixed dialog box, without maximise or minimise buttons. It is not resizable.
vbFixedToolWindow	Under Windows 3.x it behaves in the same way as the **vbFixedSingle** border. It does not have minimise or maximise buttons and is not resizable. Under Windows 95 it has a **Close** button.
vbSizableToolWindow	Under Windows 3.x it behaves in the same way as **vbSizable**. Under Windows 95 it has a **Close** button and is resizable.

- If **MinButton** is set to **True** the form has a minimise button.
- If **MaxButton** is set the form has a maximise button.
- If the **BorderStyle** property is either **vbBSNone** or **vbFixedDouble** these properties have no effect.

Using properties

You have seen how some properties of some controls can be changed, in fact all controls and forms have properties which can be seen in the Properties window.

The properties can be referred to as:

Controlname.Property

For example:

*Text1.**Enabled** = **False***

If your project has more than one form you may need to refer to a property of other forms from within a form or code module. For example, to refer to the **Caption** property of *Form1*:

> *Form1.**Caption** = "This is a new caption"*

To refer to a control's property in another form the name of the form followed by the "." operator must be used. For example:

> *Form1.Text1.**Text** = "This is new text"*

Hiding and showing forms

The application we have looked at only has one form in it. If this is the case the form will automatically be displayed when the application runs. If you have more than one form, the first form, *Form1*, will be the start-up object. You can, however, change this using the **Project | Properties** menu option and choosing the **General** page as shown in fig 6.4. The **Startup Object** is used to specify the form which is initially displayed. If no form is to be displayed on starting the application, you can specify a module which is executed first.

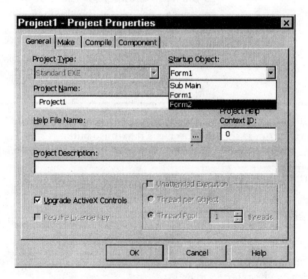

Fig 6.4 Changing the start-up form.

Loading and unloading forms

If you have more than one form in an application you need to use methods to determine which forms are displayed.

The **Load** method loads a form into memory:

> **Load** *Formname*

Load does not display the form, but it makes it available for display. Forms can be unloaded using the **Unload** method:

> **Unload** *Formname*

The Show method

The **Show** method displays a loaded form:

> *Formname.***Show** *Modestyle*

- *Modestyle* is an optional parameter. If a value of **vbModal** (0) is specified the form is modal.
- If the *Modestyle* is **vbModeless** (1) the form is non-modal. This is the default.

The **Show** method displays a form which has been loaded into memory using the **Load** method. If you use the **Show** method and specify a form which has not been loaded into memory, **Show** will carry out the load operation itself and then display the form. The only reason for using **Load** prior to **Show** is to improve the speed of the application, since the load operation can be carried out when the computer is not doing any other productive work, for example when it is waiting for user input. Loading a form is a relatively slow process since the form is stored on disk.

The Hide method

The **Hide** method is the opposite of the **Show** method and makes a form invisible:

> *Formname.***Hide**

- The **Hide** method sets the **Visible** property of the form to **False**.
- **Hide** does not unload a form from memory.
- **Hide** preserves the run-time properties of the form, while **Unload** does not.

MDI forms

MDI or Multiple Document Interface forms are child forms contained within a parent form. Fig 6.5 shows an MDI parent form with two child forms.

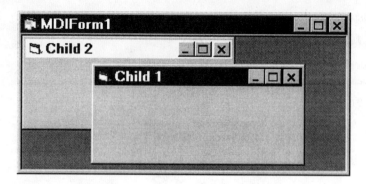

Fig 6.5 *Parent and child forms.*

In order to create an MDI application:

- Create an MDI form using the **Project | Add MDI Form** menu option.
- Create child forms using the **Project | Add Form** menu option.
- Change the **MDIChild** property of the child forms to **True**.
- To display the MDI form and the two child forms add the following code to the MDI form load event handler:

```
Private Sub MDIForm_Load( )
      Form1.Show
      Form2.Show
End Sub
```

You can only have one MDI form per application. After one MDI form has been created, the **Project | Add MDI Form** option on the menu is greyed indicating that it is unavailable.

At run-time all child forms are displayed within the MDI form, but they can be moved and sized within this area as normal. Both child and parent forms can be minimised, but when a parent form is minimised, it and all the child forms it contains are represented by a single icon.

Arranging forms

Child forms can be displayed in different ways using the **Arrange** method, for example:

```
MdForm1.Arrange vbCascade
MdForm1.Arrange vbTileHorizontal
MdForm1.Arrange vbTileVertical
```

The output from these three commands is shown in fig 6.6.

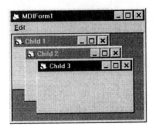 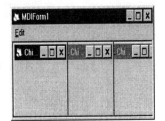 

Fig 6.6 *Arranging child forms.*

7

Displaying Text

Introduction

TextBox controls are used to display text or to allow you to enter information. Message and dialog boxes are used to give information to the application user and to take in simple responses such as Yes or No.

Most of the text that we have displayed so far has just consisted of words rather than special text such as dates, times and numbers, but Visual Basic does offer a very comprehensive set of functions for anything that you wish to display.

In this chapter you will learn about:

- Creating and using message and dialog boxes.
- Putting information onto the screen and printer.
- Controlling text font and size.
- Displaying dates, times and numbers.

The MsgBox function

Dialog boxes are a special form of window. They are very widely used for displaying warning messages or asking if you are really sure that you want an operation to occur. Dialog boxes are non-modal, that is you cannot proceed with this application until you have responded to this dialog. This does not prevent you from switching to another application.

A straight forward way of creating a dialog box is to use the **MsgBox** function.

There are five parameters for this function:

*result = **MsgBox** (text, buttons, title, helpfile, context)*

- *result* is the value returned by the function, this is optional.
- *text* is the message displayed.

- *buttons* is an optional integer value which identifies the buttons to be displayed on the dialog box.
- *title* is an optional parameter which is the string displayed at the top of the dialog box on the title bar.
- *helpfile* is an optional parameter that identifies the help file used to provide context sensitive help.
- *context* is an optional parameter which gives the help context number. This parameter can only be used if the *helpfile* parameter is specified.

For example:

> **MsgBox** *"Are you really sure?"*, **vbYesNo** + **vbCritical**, *"Warning"*

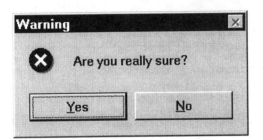

Fig 7.1 The MsgBox function.

The message box is centred in the middle of the screen.

Message box text

You can enter as much text as you want. The message box is the correct size and automatically puts in line feeds if necessary as shown in fig 7.2.

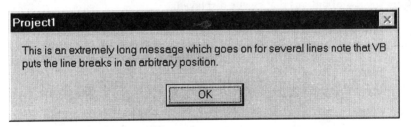

Fig 7.2 Message box text.

If you are not satisfied with the format of text, you can control it by putting ASCII line feeds explicitly in your program using the **Chr$** function, for example **Chr$**(10) is a carriage return.

```
Private Sub Command1_Click ( )
    M$ = "This is an extremely long message"
    M$ = M$ + Chr$(10) + "which goes on for several lines"
    M$ = M$ + Chr$(10) + "I have explicitly chosen where"
```

```
M$ = M$ + Chr$(10) + "the line breaks go"
    MsgBox M$
End Sub
```

This code produces the message box as shown in fig 7.3.

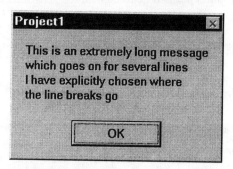

Fig 7.3 Controlling text layout using the Chr$ function.

MsgBox buttons parameter

The buttons parameter of the **MsgBox** function is more complicated than it seems at first. This single parameter is used to specify four different attributes of the dialog box:

- The buttons displayed.
- The icon displayed on the title bar.
- The default button.
- The modality of the dialog box.

There are six sets of buttons that can be displayed:

Table 7.1 MsgBox buttons.

Buttons	Value	Name
OK	0	**vbOKOnly**
OK, Cancel	1	**vbOKCancel**
Abort, Retry, Ignore	2	**vbAbortRetryIgnore**
Yes, No, Cancel	3	**vbYesNoCancel**
Yes, No	4	**vbYesNo**
Retry, Cancel	5	**vbRetryCancel**

There are 4 different icons that can be displayed:

Table 7.2 *Displaying icons.*

Icon	Value	Icon	Name
Critical	16		**vbCritical**
Question mark	32		**vbQuestion**
Exclamation mark	48		**vbExplanation**
Information	64		**vbInformation**

You can specify which of the buttons is the default:

Table 7.3 *Specifying the default button.*

Constant	Value	Meaning
vbDefaultButton1	0	First button is default.
vbDefaultButton2	256	Second button is default.
vbDefaultButton3	512	Third button is default.
vbDefaultButton4	768	Fourth button is default.

Finally you can specify if the dialog box is application or system modal:

Table 7.4 *Specifying if the dialog box is application or system modal.*

Constant	Value	Meaning
vbApplicationModal	0	Application modal.
vbSystemModal	4096	System modal.

If the dialog box is application modal (the default), this application cannot proceed until this dialog box has been responded to, but you can still switch to another application. If it is system modal, no application can proceed until a response is made. This is useful in situations where a major system wide problem has occurred, such as a defective piece of hardware.

The four aspects of the button parameter are combined to form a single argument, for example:

MsgBox "Error", vbRetryCancel + vbQuestion + vbSystemModal, "Crash"

This displays a system modal dialog box with the retry and cancel buttons and the question mark icon. The heading on the title bar is *Crash* and the text adjacent to the icon is *Error*. The dialog box produced is shown in fig 7.4.

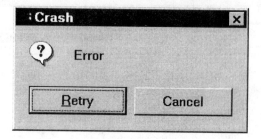

Fig 7.4 Message box text.

Getting button input

Visual Basic provides a mechanism to let your program know what button has been clicked. If you are interested in the return value you need to enclose the parameters of the **MsgBox** call in brackets as shown below.

> *Private Sub Command1_Click ( )*
> *' Must have brackets around the parameters to read the response*
> *   Response = MsgBox ("Continue", vbQuestion + vbAbortRetryIgnore)*
> *   If (Response = vbAbort) Then MyAbortRoutine( )*
> *   ...*
> *   ...*
> *End Sub*

The value of *Response* indicates the button pressed. The values which are returned are constants and can be used anywhere in your application.

Table 7.5 Getting button input.

Button Pressed	Value	Name
OK	1	vbOK
Cancel	2	vbCancel
Abort	3	vbAbort
Retry	4	vbRetry
Ignore	5	vbIgnore
Yes	6	vbYes
No	7	vbNo

When a dialog box is displayed and you do not want to proceed, the standard thing to do is press the **Escape** key. If your dialog box has a cancel button, pressing **Escape** has the same effect as clicking on the cancel button.

Getting text input from a dialog box

If you want to input some text you need to use **InputBox**.

>*InputBox (prompt, title, default, xpos, ypos, helpfile, context)*

- *prompt* is the string that is displayed in the dialog box.
- *title* is the title in the dialog box's title bar.
- *default* is the initial text placed in the **TextBox**.
- *xpos* is the distance from the left edge of the screen to the dialog box.
- *ypos* is the distance from the top of the screen to the top of the dialog box.
- *helpfile* specifies the context sensitive help file for this dialog box. If this parameter is used, *context* must also be specified.
- *context* identifies the help topic in the helpfile. The *helpfile* parameter must be used if *context* is specified.

InputBox$ always has the buttons **OK** and **Cancel**. The dialog box produced by the code below is shown in fig 7.5.

>*Prompt$ = "Install VB5 in folder"*
>*Title$ = "Setup"*
>*Default$ = "C:\Programs\VB5"*
>*Filename = **InputBox**(Prompt$, Title$, Default$)*

The parameter list for all dialog boxes can be very long, it is good practice to assign lengthy text to string variables and then to specify the strings in the function call as shown above.

If you do not specify the position of the input box, it is displayed horizontally in the centre of the screen, and about a third of the way down.

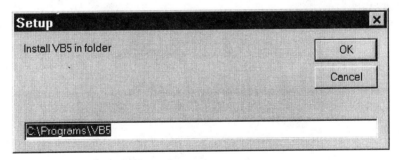

*Fig 7.5 Using **InputBox**.*

Missing optional parameters

A common problem occurs when you want to miss an optional parameter from a list. If the parameter is the last in the list you can simply omit it. The difficulty arises when you want to miss a parameter but include one that comes after it. If, for example, you wish to specify the y position of an input box, but not the x position. You do this by omitting the *xpos* parameter but including the comma separator before the *ypos* parameter, for example:

*Response = **InputBox**("File name?", "File Input", "Project.txt", , ypos)*

Controlling fonts and font characteristics

Textual attributes of **Label** and **TextBox** controls affect all the text. It is not possible to make only a part of the text bold unless you use a **RichTextBox** custom control. The easiest way to control the font of a label or text box is at design time, however you can control all of the characteristics at run-time by using the **Font** property.

If you change the **Font** property of any container, including a form, the default **Font** properties placed in that container will be changed.

In fig 7.6 when the buttons marked *Bold* or *Italic* are pressed, the text *Chameleon* changes. The text on the buttons themselves also changes. Pressing one of the buttons again reverses the change. The code is shown below:

```
Private Sub Command1_Click( )
    Text1.Font.Bold = Not Text1.Font.Bold
    Command1.Font.Bold = Text1.Font.Bold
End Sub

Private Sub Command2_Click( )
    Text1.Font.Italic = Not Text1.Font.Italic
    Command2.Font.Italic = Text1.Font.Italic
End Sub
```

*Fig 7.6 Using the **Font** property.*

In addition to making text italic or bold you can control every aspect of the font.

Table 7.6 *The **Font** property.*

Property	Type
FontName	string
FontSize	integer - in points
FontBold	boolean
FontItalic	boolean
FontStrikethru	boolean
FontUnderline	boolean
FontTransparent	boolean

Since not all properties are supported by all fonts it is advisable to set the **FontName** property first which will return the name of available fonts. To find out all of the fonts available for your system you can use the application shown in fig 7.7.

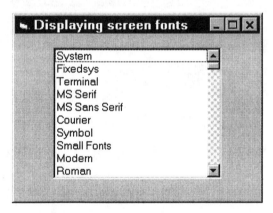

Fig 7.7 *Displaying screen fonts.*

This **ListBox** is filled with all of the available fonts in response to a form load event. The code is shown below:

```
Private Sub Form_Load( )
    For c = 0 To Screen.FontCount - 1
        List1.AddItem Screen.Fonts(c)
    Next c
End Sub
```

FontCount gives the number of available fonts, these are added to a list box using the **AddItem** method. If you wish to see which fonts are available for your printer you should use the **Printer** object. In this example, all you have to do is substitute the word **Printer** for **Screen**.

Using the Print method

Visual Basic also allows you to display information anywhere on the form using the **Print** method. **Print** places text at the current position of the cursor and in the current font and size. For example:

```
Private Sub Form_Click ( )
    For c= 8 To 20 Step 2
        Form1.FontSize = c
        Print "Bigger and bigger"
    Next c
End Sub
```

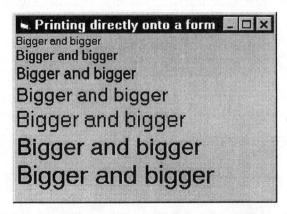

Fig 7.8 Changing the font size.

Formatting numbers dates and times

You can rely on the Visual Basic defaults when displaying numbers, dates or times, but Visual Basic does offer very extensive facilities for controlling the way in which these are printed. For clarity, the **Print** method has been used to illustrate how these formats are used, but they can equally be used to build up a string which can be assigned, for example, to the **Text** property of a **TextBox** control.

Number format

Format$ and **Format** functions allow you to specify the way in which characters are displayed

Format[$] (expression[, fmt$])

fmt$ describes how the number (in *expression*) is to be formatted when displayed.

Visual Basic supplies a number of standard formats for displaying numbers:

Table 7.7 Number formats.

Number Formats	Description
general number	Numbers displayed with no thousand separator.
currency	Displays with a thousand separator; negative numbers in brackets and two digits after the decimal point.
fixed	At least one digit before the point and two after.
standard	Similar to **fixed** but inserts a thousand separator.
percent	Similar to **fixed** but multiplies the value by 100, and appends the percent sign (%).
scientific	Displays the number in standard scientific notation.

```
Private Sub Form_Click ( )
    Value = 123456.789
    Print "No particular format   : "; Format$(Value)
    Print "The general format     : "; Format$(Value, "general number")
    Print "The currency format    : "; Format$(Value, "currency")
    Print "The standard format    : "; Format$(Value, "standard")
    Print "The scientific format  : "; Format$(Value, "scientific")
End Sub
```

If more than one item is to be printed, as above, the items are separated by semicolons. If a mono-spaced font such as Courier is used, the numbers will line up, however, if you use a variable spaced font such as Times Roman you will need to use the **Tab** function to ensure that the numbers are in line.

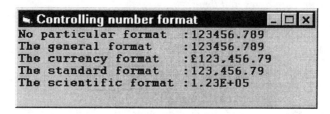

Fig 7.9 Formatting numbers.

Boolean operators are either zero or non zero.

Table 7.8 Boolean formats.

Binary	Description
Yes/No	Any non-zero value displays **Yes**. A zero value displays **No**.
True/False	Any non-zero value displays **False**. A zero value displays **True**.
On/Off	Any non-zero value displays **On**. A zero value displays **Off**.

These can be displayed using **Format$** and the boolean operators given in table 7.8.

Custom formats

Visual Basic also allows you to create your own formats using a set of symbols shown in table 7.9:

Table 7.9 Custom formats.

Symbol	Description
0	Digit place holder. This requires a leading or trailing 0 in this position if padding is necessary to fill this position.
#	Digit place holder. Digits may be printed here. Leading/ trailing 0's are not displayed.
.	Decimal place holder.
,	Thousands separator.
-+$£() space	Literal characters. These characters are entered into the formatted string exactly as they appear.

```
Print Format$(876.34, "00000.0000")      ' 00876.3400
Print Format$(876.34, "#####.####")      ' 876.34
Print Format$(876.345, "$##.00")         ' $876.35 (to 2 dec. places)
```

Date and time format

Visual Basic offers a range of standard formats for displaying dates and times which are used with **Format[$]**.

Table 7.10 Displaying dates and times.

Date Formats	Description
general date	Uses the short date and time formats dependent on the information in the expression field.
long date	Displays the entire month in textual form, for example, 1 June 1997.
medium date	The month is displayed in abbreviated textual forms and the year abbreviated, for example, 1 Jun-97.
short date	The month is in number form and the year abbreviated, for example, 1/6/97.

The **Now** function returns the current date and time.

```
Private Sub Form_Click ( )
    Print "No particular format"; Tab(23); Format$(Now)
    Print "General date format"; Tab(23); Format$(Now, "general date")
    Print "Long date format"; Tab(23); Format$(Now, "long date")
    Print "Medium date format"; Tab(23); Format$(Now, "medium date")
```

> **Print** *"Short date format"; **Tab**(23); **Format$**(Now, "short date")*
> **End Sub**

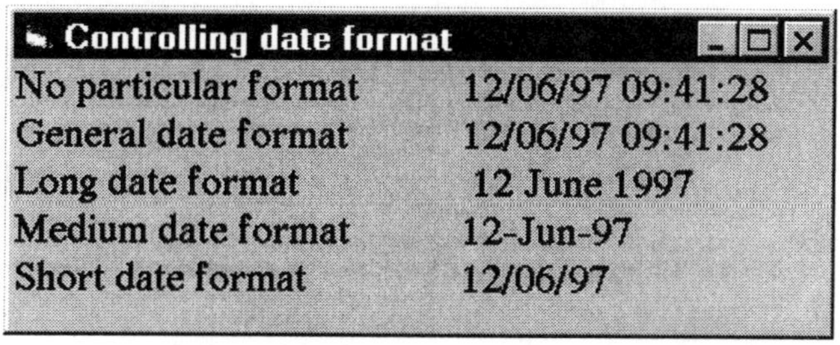

```
 Controlling date format          _ □ ×
No particular format      12/06/97 09:41:28
General date format       12/06/97 09:41:28
Long date format          12 June 1997
Medium date format        12-Jun-97
Short date format         12/06/97
```

Fig 7.10 Formatting dates.

Similarly there are a range of standard formats for printing the time:

Table 7.11 *Time formats.*

Time Formats	Description
long time	The Regional Settings page of the Control Panel describes the format used for hours, minutes and seconds and features such as separators between hours, minutes and seconds and AM/PM indicators used.
medium time	The medium time format displays the hours and minutes and the AM/PM designator.
short time	The short time format displays the hours and seconds in 24 hour format, separated by the character specified in the Regional Settings page of the Control Panel.

> **Private Sub** *Form_Click ( )*
>   **Print** *"No particular format"; **Tab**(23); **Format$**(Now)*
>   **Print** *"Long time format"; **Tab**(23); **Format$**(Now, "long time")*
>   **Print** *"Medium time format"; **Tab**(23); **Format$**(Now, "medium time")*
>   **Print** *"Short time format"; **Tab**(23); **Format$**(Now, "short time")*
> **End Sub**

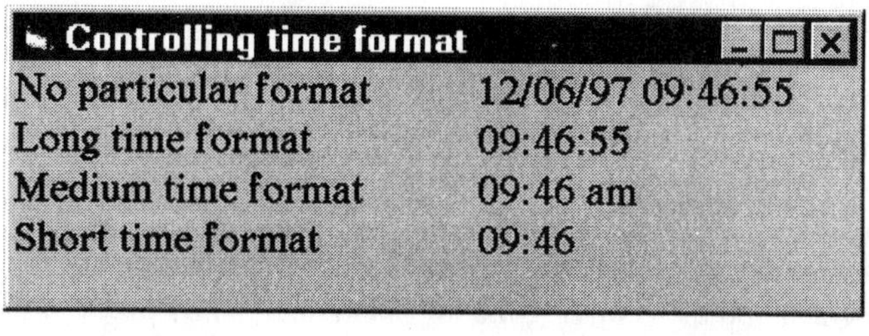

```
 Controlling time format          _ □ ×
No particular format      12/06/97 09:46:55
Long time format          09:46:55
Medium time format        09:46 am
Short time format         09:46
```

Fig 7.11 Formatting time.

Your application may look slightly different to the one shown in fig 7.11, depending on how you have set up the Regional Settings page of the Control Panel.

Writing to a printer

The printer can be addressed in two ways, either:

- Collect the information on the **Printer** object and then print the **Printer** object.
- Assemble the information on a form and then print the form.

The Printer object

You can print directly onto a form using the **Print** method. Visual Basic supports a drawing space called the **Printer** object which is device independent. You write to this drawing space using the **Print**, **Line** and all the usual methods which are used for displaying on the screen. When you are ready to print the page you have built up, you call the **NewPage** method. The page size of the **Printer** object is defined by its **Height** and **Width** properties.

> *Printer.NewPage*

NewPage maintains page numbers that can be used for creating numbered pages, this is saved in the property **Page**. When you are ready to print out the last page you call the **EndDoc** method, if you forget to do this, there is an automatic **EndDoc** if the **Printer** object is not empty.

The example below prints *Page number 1* on the first page and *Page number 2* on the second page, before closing the printer object.

> *Printer.Print "Page number " + Printer.Page*
> *Printer.NewPage*
> *Printer.Print "Page number " + Printer.Page*
> *Printer.EndDoc*

The PrintForm method

The **PrintForm** method prints the specified form. If no form is specified the form which holds the focus is printed.

> *Form1.Printform*

The **PrintForm** method relies on the application assembling the information on a form on the screen and then copying the information, pixel by pixel, to the printer. The output can be disappointing on a high quality printer because the printer resolution, typically 600 pixels per inch, may be much greater than the typical screen resolution of 100 pixels per inch.

8

Declaring and Using Variables

Introduction

We have used some of Visual Basic's data types without looking too closely at the range of data which is available or the operators which act upon the data.

In this chapter you will learn about:

- The different data types.
- The range of data types.
- Declaring variables.
- Using the right operators.

Declaring variables

One of the most common mistakes in Visual Basic is to slightly mis-spell the name of a variable. This does not cause a syntax error, but the program does not behave as expected. One way around this is to declare the name and type of variables prior to their first use, the **Dim** statement is used for this, for example:

> **Dim** *Value As Integer, Total As Single*

The general form is:

> **Dim** *identifier As type, identifier As type*

It is a good idea to make variable declaration mandatory by either:

- Selecting the **Tools | Options** menu option and to select the **Editor** page as shown in fig 8.1.

- If you only want to force explicit declarations in one module, put the following line into the declarations section of the module:

Option Explicit

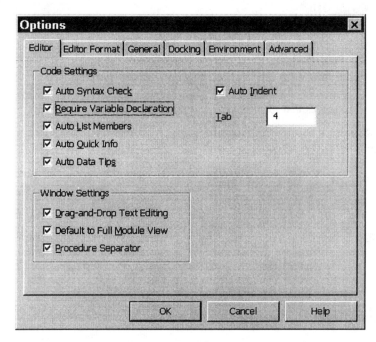

Fig 8.1 The Editor page.

Naming conventions

Variable names must conform to these rules:

- They must begin with a letter.
- They must contain only letters, numbers and the underscore characters.
- They must be 40 characters or less.

Static variables

There are a number of other issues to be considered when you are declaring a variable. A variable declared within a procedure is initialised every time the procedure is entered. However, if you want a variable to retain its value and not be re-initialised the **Static** keyword must be used in place of **Dim**.

Static *identifier **As** type*

for example:

>   **Static** *MyName* **As String**

Variables scope

Variables can be declared in modules, forms or procedures:

- A variable declared in a procedure is only available for use within that procedure, even if it has been declared **Static**.
- A variable declared within the general section of a form has scope throughout that form.

The scope of variables declared at module level depends on the keyword used to declare it:

- If a variable is declared with **Dim** it has scope throughout the module.
- If a variable is declared as **Global** it is available throughout the program:

>   **Global** *identifier* **As** *type*

The **Dim** keyword is replaced, for example:

>   **Global** *YourName* **As String**

Variable types

Visual Basic offers an extensive range of twelve data types.

Table 8.1 Data types.

Type	Size in bytes	Suffix
Boolean	2	No suffix.
Byte	1	No suffix.
Currency	8	@
Date	8	No suffix.
Decimal	14	No suffix.
Integer	2	%
Long	4	&
Object	4	No suffix.
Single	4	!
Double	8	#
String	Dependent on string size.	$
Variant	Dependent on type of data stored.	None.

If these data types are not sufficient you can even define your own.

There are two ways of defining the type of a variable explicitly, you can either use **Dim** or its variants or for some types you can follow the name by a suffix, for example, **Value%** is an integer, while **MyLine$** is a string.

The Boolean data type

The **Boolean** type is used to store a **True** / **False** or **Yes** / **No** type variable.

The Byte data type

This is an unsigned data type which can hold values between 0 and 255.

The Currency data type

As the name suggests this type should be used for calculations involving money. There are 4 digits on the right of the decimal point and up to 14 digits on the left.

The Date data type

The **Date** type does not have a suffix, but when assigning a date to a variable of this type, the date is enclosed between two # characters, for example:

> *PamsBirthday = #15/7/60#*

A useful function is **Now** which returns the current date and time, for example:

> *TheDateToday = **Now***

The date tomorrow can be calculated as:

> *Tomorrow = **Now** + 1*

or

> *Tomorrow = TheDateToday + 1*

The Decimal data type

This is a new data type in version 5, which has been introduced in response to the demands of users who are performing extensive mathematical processing. It is the largest and the most accurate of the floating point data types.

The Integer data type

The most commonly used data type. Integers should be used wherever possible, in preference to floating point numbers, because operations on them are fast and the rounding problems of the single, double and decimal types does not occur. The % suffix indicates an integer without a **Dim** statement, for example:

MyInteger% = 37

The Long data type

The range of integers is limited. For situations where a greater range is required the **Long** data type should be used.

The Object data type

This data type is used to hold any object reference. Objects are dealt with in detail in chapter 12.

The Single data type

This is a floating point type which should be used where accuracy is not paramount. Operations are still relatively quick on this type, although much slower than on either of the integer types.

The Double data type

This is a more accurate floating point data type, which should be used in preference to **Single** where accuracy is more important.

The String data type

This data type is used to contain a sequence of characters. One of the strengths of Visual Basic is the way in which you can use this data type, for example:

MyString$ = "You can add strings together in Visual Basic "
MyString$ = MyString$ + " like this"

You can also use the & operator to concatenate strings, although + is more widely used.

The Variant data type

The **Variant** data type takes on the form of the data which it is asked to store. For example, if a string is assigned to a **Variant** type, the **Variant** type takes on the **String** data type. If it is assigned a numeric value it takes on that type and can be used in calculations.

Variants should be used with great care.

Range of data types

The **Single** and **Long** types are real, floating point types which approximate to the number being represented. In an accounting system the **Currency** type should be used which does not introduce rounding errors.

Table 8.2 The range of data types.

Type	Most Negative	Most Positive
Byte	0	255
Boolean	not applicable.	not applicable.
Integer	-32,768	32,767
Long	-2,147,483,648	2,147,483,647
Double	-1.797 693 134 862 32 E308	1.797 693 134 862 32 E308
Currency	-922,337,203,685,477 ·5808	922,337,203,685,477 ·5807
Decimal	79228162414264337593543950335	79228162414264337593543950335
Date	earliest : January 1 100.	latest : December 31 9999.
Object	not applicable.	not applicable.
Single	-3.402 823 E38	3.402 823 E38
Variant (numbers)	same as double.	same as double.
Variant (string)	not applicable.	not applicable.
String	not applicable.	approx. 65,400 characters.

Converting between data types

If care is not paid to the types of variables problems can occur. Fortunately there is a wide range of functions available which allow you to convert one data type to another as shown in table 8.3.

If the function cannot perform the conversion, for example if **CDate** is used and the variable is not in an appropriate format, an error will occur. You can test for a date type using the **IsDate** function, which returns a **Boolean** indication. Similar functions are available for testing other data types.

CCur should always be used in preference to **Val** for **Currency** types, since it recognises international currency settings as specified on your computer.

Table 8.3 *Functions for converting between data types.*

Function	Return type	Function	Return type
CBool	Boolean	CInt	Int
CByte	Byte	CLng	Long
CCur	Currency	CSng	Single
CDate	Date	CVar	Variant
CDbl	Double	CStr	String
CDec	Decimal		

Int and Fix

CInt and **CLng** always round to the nearest even number, for example, 2.9 rounds to 4 while 5.2 rounds to 6. There is often some confusion between these functions and the **Int** and **Fix** functions, both of which truncate a number, for example 7.9 is truncated to 7.

The difference between **Int** and **Fix** is in the way in which they deal with negative numbers, **Int** will convert to the first negative integer greater than or equal to the number, for example -7.3 produces -8, while **Fix** will truncate -7.3 to -7.

Arithmetic operations

Much of the use of operators is similar to other programming languages, however it is worthwhile reviewing as there may be a few surprises.

There are seven arithmetic operations.

Table 8.4 *The arithmetic operators.*

Operator	Action	Example
+	Addition.	$1 + 5 = 6$
-	Subtraction.	$8 - 5 = 3$
*	Multiplication.	$2.6 * 3 = 7.8$
/	Division.	$23 / 2 = 11.5$
^	Exponentiation.	$3 \wedge 2 = 9$
\	Integer Division.	$6 \setminus 1.6 = 3$
Mod	Modulus, returns the remainder after integer division.	$7 \textbf{ Mod } 2 = 1$

The comparison operators

The standard set of comparison operators are provided.

Table 8.5 The comparison operators.

Operator	Action
=	Equal.
<	Less than.
>	Greater than.
<=	Less than or equal.
>=	Greater than or equal.
<>	Not equal.

These operators can be used on strings as well as numeric values.

Arrays

The most common form of data structure is the array, which is a way of collecting together similar items of the same data type. For example, a list of employee salaries can be saved as a one dimensional array of type **Currency**. While, for example, a holiday chart can be saved as a two-dimensional array. Unlike most languages, Visual Basic also allows you to amend the dimensions of arrays at run-time.

Declaring arrays

Before an array can be used it must be declared using the **Dim** statement.

> *Dim name (subscripts) [As type] [, ...]*

The simplest arrays have only one dimension, for example:

> *Dim MyList(5)*

This defines a one dimensional array with 6 elements, *MyList(0)* to *MyList(5)*. The statement:

> *Dim MyList(0 To 5)*

is equivalent.

Arrays can have up to 60 dimensions, when declaring a multi-dimensional array, all dimensions must be specified If a lower bound is not explicitly stated, the lower limit is zero. The following are all equivalent:

> *Dim MyArray (7, 2)*
> *Dim MyArray (0 To 7, 0 To 2)*
> *Dim MyArray (7, 0 To 2)*

It is important to choose a style that you like and to stick with it for consistency.

Changing array dimensions

Visual Basic allows you to change the size, but not the type of arrays at run-time using the **ReDim** statement.

>   **Dim** *Range(10 **To** 20) **As Integer***
>
>   ...
>
>   ...
>
>   **ReDim** *Range (15 **To** 30)*

The **ReDim** statement changes the number of elements so that the first is 15 and the last is 30.

If you want to preserve values already in the array, you need to use the optional keyword **Preserve**, otherwise they are erased.

>   **Dim** *Range (10 **To** 20) **As Integer***
>
>   ...
>
>   ...
>
>   **ReDim Preserve** *Range (10 **To** 30)*

If you use **Preserve**, you can only change the dimension of the final element.

User-defined data types

Sometimes it is useful to group together information, for example, if you are maintaining employee records in a company:

Table 8.6 User-defined data types.

Name	Age	Salary
Jim	34	29,000
Sally	28	58,000
Duncan	57	37,000

Each row of the table can be grouped together using a user-defined data type defined by the **Type** Statement.

>   **Type** *Specification*
>   *Processor **As String***
>   *MemorySize **As Integer***
>   *Cost **As Currency***
>   **End Type**
>
>   **Dim** *Computers(5) **As Specification***

- You can refer to the second computer's cost by *Computer(1).Cost*.
- If user-defined types are used within an array, they cannot be redefined at run-time using **ReDim**.

The Erase statement

If you want to free the memory space taken up by a dynamic array, you can use the **Erase** statement, for example:

> **Dim** *MyArray(10 to 20) As Integer*
>
> ...
>
> **Erase** *MyArray*

For static arrays the space is not recovered. Instead **Erase** sets the elements of the array to "empty" values.

- For numeric arrays, **Erase** sets each element to zero.
- String static arrays, **Erase** sets each element to an empty string ("").
- Array of user-defined types, **Erase** sets all elements to 0, including fixed string elements.

9

Controlling Program Flow

Introduction

Visual Basic has a comprehensive set of language features that allow your program to follow different paths through your code depending on the value of data variables. You have already seen this happen using **If** statements, but there is a far more comprehensive set of language constructs than this.

In this chapter you will learn about:

- **If, Then, Else** statements.
- **Select, Case** statements.
- **Switch** statements.
- Looping statements.

Types of program control

There are 3 constructs which can be used to control program flow:

- **If...Then** statement.
- **Select Case** structure.
- **GoTo** statement.

These are similar to most modern languages; however, there are a few important features unique to Visual Basic.

The If...Then...Else statement

This statement exists in two forms, the single and multi line. The simplest form of the **If...Then** statement is the single line:

*If condition **Then** statement*

For example:

*If MemorySize < 16 **Then MsgBox** "Not ideal for Windows"*

If your memory size is less than 16Mb a message box is displayed stating that your system is *Not ideal for Windows*. If *MemorySize* is 16 or more then no action is taken. An **Else** clause can be added:

*If condition **Then** statement **Else** statement*

For example:

*If (MemorySize < 16) **Then MsgBox** "Not ideal" **Else MsgBox** "Fine"*

The multi-line version of the statement is a little more complicated

*If condition **Then***
    statements
Else If** condition **Then
    statements
Else
    statements
End If

For example:

*If (ProcessorSpeed < 133) **Then***
    ***MsgBox** "Slow"*
Else
    ***MsgBox** "Fast"*
End If

Nested Ifs

If statements can be nested to make multiple levels of decision, for example:

*If (MemorySize < 16) **Then***
    *If (ProcessorSpeed <= 133) **Then***
        *If (DiskSize < 1000) **Then***
            ***MsgBox** "Too slow for Windows"*
        End If

```
    End If
End If
```

If possible avoid using nested **Ifs** of this type; they are very confusing. A better coding for the above example would be:

```
If (MemorySize < 16) And (ProcessorSpeed <= 133) And (DiskSize<1000)
Then
    MsgBox "Too slow for Windows"
End If
```

The **And** and **Or** clauses need to be on the same line as the **If** and **Then** words.

The Else If clause

Multiple **Else** clauses can also be used, for example:

```
If HoursWorked <= 20  Then
    MsgBox "Taking it easy"
Else If HoursWorked >= 80 Then
    MsgBox "Slow down"
End If
```

You can have as many **Else If** clauses as you want.

The Select Case structure

The **Select Case** construction is useful when there are several consequences dependent on the result of one expression.

The syntax of **Select Case** is:

```
Select Case testexpression
    Case expressionlist1
        statementblock1
    Case expressionlist2
        statementblock2

    ...
    [Case Else
        statementblockn]
End Select
```

At each **Case** statement, four different types of expression lists can used:

- A string or numeric expression.
- An explicit value.
- A range using the keyword **To.**
- A conditional range using the keyword **Is.**

For example:

```
Select Case Speed
    Case 0, 1, 2
        MsgBox "Driving a little slow"
    Case 3 To 30
        MsgBox "Driving within legal limits"
    Case 31 To 40
        MsgBox "Driving a little too fast"
    Case Is > 40
        MsgBox "Driving much too fast"
End Select
```

- **Case** 0,1,2 means if the *Speed* is 0, 1, or 2 display the message *Driving a little slow*.
- **Case 3 To** 30 applies if *Speed* is in the range 3-30.
- **Case Is** > 40 applies if *Speed* is greater than 40.

The GoTo statement

GoTo unconditionally transfers control to a specified label. The **GoTo** statement has proved to be the most unpopular statement in modern programming languages as you can usually remove the need for a **GoTo** statement using other programming statements. It is usually good practice to avoid using this statement, however it can be useful if a error occurs to simply jump straight to the error handler.

> *GoTo label*

Labels are identifiers with a colon suffix.
For example:

```
...
If ErrorNumber <> 0 Then GoTo ErrorHandler
...
...
ErrorHandler:
```

The *ErrorHandler* label is indicated by an appended colon.

Looping

Looping constructs are used when the same set of steps has to be carried out many times. There is usually a counter which indicates how many times the loop is executed or a test that is made every time the loop is executed to see if the program should exit the loop again. There are three looping constructs in Visual Basic:

- **Do...Loop**
- **While...Wend**
- **For...Next**

The Do...While clause

The **Do**...**Loop** construct allows you to execute a block of code if the specified condition is met.

> ***Do While*** *condition*
> > *statements*
> ***Loop***

For example:

> *FileFound =* ***False***
> ***Do While*** *FileFound =* ***False***
> > *GetFileName( )*
> > *FileFound = OpenFile( )*
> ***Loop***

Another form of the **Do**…**While** statement is to have the **While** condition at the end of the loop.

> ***Do***
> > *Statements*
> ***Loop While*** *condition*

For example:

> ***Do***
> > *GetFileName( )*
> > *FileFound = OpenFile( )*
> ***Loop While*** *FileFound =* ***False***

The difference between this example and the previous one is that in this form the loop will always be executed once - since the test is made at the end of the loop. In this case it is more efficient since we always want to execute the loop once and there is no need to assign the *FileFound* boolean to **False** prior to entering the loop.

The Do...Until clause

This looping construct is very similar in function to the **Loop**...**While** construct.

> ***Do Until*** *condition*
> > *statements*
> ***Loop***

For example:

> *FileFound = **False***
> ***Do Until** FileFound <> **False***
> > *GetFileName( )*
> > *FileFound = OpenFile( )*
> ***Loop***

A variant of this construct is to put the condition at the end of the loop.

> ***Do***
> > *statements*
> ***Loop Until** condition*

For example:

> ***Do***
> > *GetFileName( )*
> > *FileFound = OpenFile( )*
> ***Loop Until** FileFound <> **False***

This is functionally the same as the first example except that the loop is always executed once.

Exit Do statement

Loops can be aborted using the **Exit Do** construct but it is not good programming practice and can make programs difficult to understand and to debug.

> *attempts = 0*
> ***Do***
> > *GetFileName( )*
> > *FileFound = OpenFile( )*
> > *attempts = attempts + 1*
> > ***If** attempts > 10 **Then Exit Do***
> ***Loop While** FileFound = **False***

If there have been ten attempts, the **Exit Do** construct exits the loop and jumps to the line after the **Loop** statement. If there are nested loops the **Exit Do** construct jumps to the next loop level not out of all of the nested loops.

The While... Wend clause

The **While...Wend** clause is functionally the same as the **Do While**...**Loop** form of **Do**...**Loop** and is similar in syntax to **While** loops in other languages.

> *FileFound = **False***
> ***While** FileFound = **False***

```
        GetFileName( )
        FileFound = OpenFile( )
    Wend
```

The **Exit Do** facility is not available in **While...Wend** and has no equivalent.

The For...Next construct

The **For**...**Next** construct has an integral loop counter. The syntax is:

```
    For counter = start To end [Step increment]
    [statementblock]
    [Exit For]
    [statementblock]
    Next [counter [, counter]]
```

For example:

```
    For Count = 1 To NumberOfMembers
    PrintLetter( )
    Next Count
```

This prints a letter to each member and automatically increments the loop counter *Count*. The amount by which the counter is changed every time it loops is indicated by the **Step** construct. The default step value is 1.

```
    For Count = 0 To 10 Step 2
    MsgBox Count
    Next Count
```

This prints out 0, 2, 4, 6, 8, 10 and the loop value is changed until it exceeds the terminating value.

The **Step** value can also be negative in which case the counter is decremented.

```
    For Count = 10 To 2 Step -3
    MsgBox Count
    Next Count
```

This prints out the values 10, 7, 4.

At the start of the next loop the value of *Count* is 1; as it is less than the terminating value, the loop therefore terminates.

Terminating For loops

Next can be used to terminate several loops at the same time by listing several variable counters.

```
        For X = 1 To 10
            For Y = 1 To 20
                Value[X, Y] = True
        Next Y, X
```

Exit For

The **Exit For** construct can only be used from within a **For** loop and is a way of leaving the loop immediately.

```
        Sum = 0
        For  Count = 1 To 10
            Value = GetInput( )
            If Value < 0  Then Exit For
            Sum = Value + Sum
        Next Count
```

One of the major run-time problems when developing an application is that endless loops can occur if the end conditions are never met. It is not advisable to modify the loop counter within the loop for this reason.

10
Procedures and Functions

Introduction

It is a standard practice in all programming languages to break your application down into a set of small units. Visual Basic has, in common with most other languages, both procedures and functions, which have slightly different properties.

In this chapter you will learn about:

- Event and general procedures.
- **Sub** procedures.
- **Function** procedures.

Event procedures

You have already seen and used a lot of event procedures. If you want to add a new event procedure to your form:

- Display the code window.
- Select the object you want to want to create the event for from the object list.
- Select the event from the list of available events for that object from the events list.

This is shown in fig 10.1.

The general form of an event procedures is:

> *Private Sub* controlname_eventname( )
>   *statement block*
> *End Sub*

An event procedure name comprises:

- The control's name.
- An underscore.
- The event name.

If, for example, a command button is called *Cancel,* that is its **Name** property is *Cancel,* and a mouse button is clicked on that button then a **Click** event occurs and the event procedure is called *Cancel_Click.*

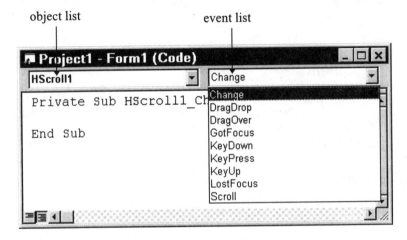

Fig 10.1 Creating event procedures.

Event procedures are always **Sub** procedures not **Function** procedures. **Sub** procedures do not return a value.

General procedures

A procedure that is not invoked in response to an event is called a general procedure:

- Events often cause similar operations to be performed. A single general procedure could be called by a variety of event procedures - avoiding duplication of code.
- If a general procedure is defined in a form module it can be called by any of the event procedures in that form.
- If a general procedure is to be called from anywhere in the application it must be in a code module, that is a BAS file.

The scope of event and general procedures

All executable code is either in a general procedure or an event procedure.

- Each event procedure is associated with a particular form.
- The same application can have many event procedures with the same name - but each associated with different forms.

General procedures can be defined in either the general section of either a form or a code module.

- A general procedure defined in a form can only be called from within that form.
- A general procedure defined in the general section of a code module can be called from anywhere within the application.

Passing arguments

The syntax for a **Sub** procedure is :

> **Private Sub** *ProcedureName (argument_list)*
>   *statements*
> **End Sub**

The argument list is a list of argument names separated by commas:

> *[**ByVal**] variablename [( )] [**As** type]*

- The **ByVal** keyword indicates that the parameter is being passed by value not by reference.
- The *type* specifier gives the type of the variable being passed.

The procedure shown below is called *Update* and it passes two values called *Index* which is an **Integer** and *Value* which is of type **Single**.

> **Private Sub** *Update (Index **As Integer**, **ByVal** Value **As Single**)*

This can be called, for example, by the statement:

> *Update 15, 39.5*

Function procedures

The syntax for a **Function** procedure is:

> **Function** *ProcedureName (argument_list) [**As** type]*
>   *Statements*
> **End Function**

This operates in exactly the same way as the **Sub** procedure except for three differences:

- Brackets must always be used around the arguments.
- Function procedures have data types, just as variables do. This controls the type of return value.
- A value is returned by assigning the function name itself.

A user-defined function procedure can be used in the same way as any of the built-in Visual Basic functions. For example:

Function Biggest (A ,B ,C) *As Single*
    A = Biggest
    if B > Biggest *Then* Biggest = B
    if C > Biggest *Then* Biggest = C
End Function

This can be called, for example, by the statement:

Answer = Biggest (7.5, 8.3, -67.3)

11
Debugging

Introduction

All software has bugs in it. Even if you write an application without any bugs, it is not possible to prove that it is completely without error. Some bugs are more subtle and difficult to find than others, even applications such as Visual Basic itself must contain bugs. Most of these will never cause you any problems. The best that programmers can do is to test their applications thoroughly. Visual Basic provides some debugging tools to help you find any errors in your applications.

In this chapter you will find out:

- What debugging is.
- How the Quick Info feature works.
- How to debug applications.
- The key features of the debug menu bar.
- How to trap errors.

What is debugging?

All of the applications that you write will not work the first time! There are two main types of errors:

- Syntax and semantic errors. These are caused when, for example, you mistype the name of a reserved word (**Fir** instead of **For**). This sort of error may occur when Visual Basic is unable to execute a line of your application because of some internal consistency, such as assigning a string identifier to an integer. These errors are fairly easy to find.
- Logic errors are much harder to correct. These are caused by some fault in your thinking when creating the application. Logic errors may cause Visual Basic to report an error, while others will simply give the incorrect answer.

We are going to look briefly at dealing with syntax errors, but since these are much easier to deal with we are going to concentrate on dealing with logic errors.

Syntax errors and Quick Info

One improvement introduced in version 5, is that IntelliSense has been included. When you are typing code, Visual Basic provides hints or tips which help you to write syntactically correct code. There are three types of helpful hints which IntelliSense provided:

- Parameters for methods and functions.
- Properties and methods of an object.
- A list of acceptable constants.

In fig 11.1, this Quick Info feature indicates that the **Val** function requires a single string as its input parameter and returns a double value.

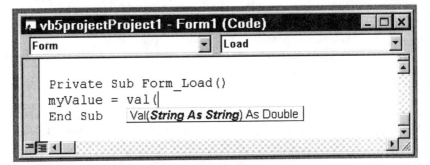

Fig 11.1 Method and function parameters.

When you type the name of any object the properties of that object are listed, as shown in fig 11.2.

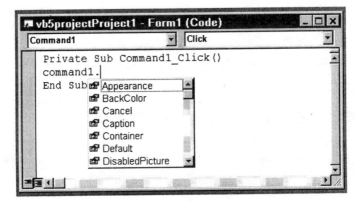

Fig 11.2 Object properties.

When you are intending to assign the property of a object, a list of possible values is displayed as shown in fig 11.3. If you wish to insert one of the possible options into your code, click on that option, or move to it by using the arrowed keys and press the **Tab** key.

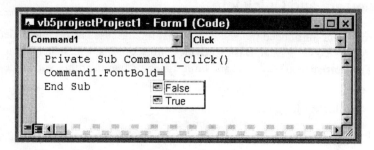

Fig 11.3 List of acceptable constants.

You can turn the IntelliSense feature off using the **Editor** page of the **Tools |**
Options menu. Click on the Quick Info check box so that it is not checked.

If you have turned this feature off, you can still use it occasionally by choosing the **Quick Info** or **Parameter Info** options from the edit speed menu.

Logic errors

Logic errors only become apparent at run-time, so the key to finding logic errors is to be able to stop the application at specified points and to find out what is happening at those points, in order to identify the point at which things started to go wrong. Visual Basic offers an extremely good set of debugging tools which help you to do this.

Using breakpoints

When you put a breakpoint into your application, it will stop executing when it reaches that point. When you are in break mode you can examine the values of identifiers and even edit code before the application continues executing.

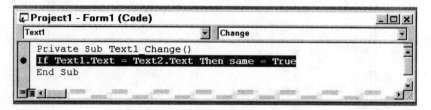

Fig 11.4 Inserting a breakpoint.

To insert a breakpoint in your code, either click on the grey bar on the left of the line, or press **F9**. Breakpoints can be turned off in the same way. A breakpoint is indicated by a dot on the far left of the line, and the line itself is highlighted as shown in fig 11.4.

You can also cause an application to break by putting a **Stop** statement in your code. You can halt an executing application by pressing **Ctrl+Break**; the application breaks after executing the current line it is on.

You can find out details of a breakpoint by pressing **Shift+F9** or choosing the **View | Quick Watch** menu option while at a breakpoint. The Quick Watch window is shown in fig 11.5.

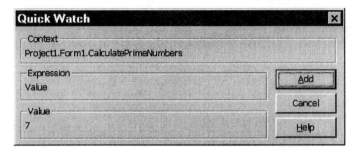

Fig 11.5 Inserting a breakpoint.

Displaying the value of variables

When a program has broken you can display the values of any variables which are in scope. If you move the cursor over the variable its value is displayed. In fig 11.6 the variable *Value* is currently 15.

```
Private Sub CalculatePrimeNumbers()
    limit = 100
    For Value = 7 To limit Step 2
        prime = True
        For c = 3 To Value / 2 Step 2
            If Value / c <> Int(Value / c) Then
                prime = False          Value = 15
        Next c
    Next Value
```

Fig 11.6 Displaying variable values.

Note in fig 11.6 that there appear to be two breakpoints on consecutive lines, in fact there is a continuation character at the end of the first line, indicating that this is a long line which is continued onto a second line.

An alternative way of displaying values is to use the Immediate window. When you are at a breakpoint, if you click on the Immediate window to give it the focus you can display the value of any variables in scope by using **Print** or ? for example:

> *Print c*
> *?c*

Both lines have the same effect; the current value of the variable *c* is displayed.

Changing code in break mode

When you are in break mode you can amend your code, simply by going to the appropriate place in the code window and typing the lines you wish to insert, or by deleting or changing existing lines.

Version 5 removes some of the limitations of what you could do in break mode in version 4. You can now load a form providing that the form is closed, and you can also call one of your own procedures.

If you want to execute a line of code once only, you can type this in the immediate window. When you press **Return**, the line is executed.

Continuing and stopping

After examining the values of variables you can continue executing your code in any of the following ways:

- Press **F5.**
- Select the **Run | Continue** menu option.
- Press the **Run** icon on the toolbar.

If you want to restart the application from the beginning:

- Press **Shift+F5.**
- Select the **Run | Restart** menu option.

Stepping

Sometimes if you are unsure about the order in which your statements are executed because there is complex branching in your code, it is useful to be able to execute the code one line at a time. When you are in break mode, you can step by pressing **F8** or by choosing the **Debug | Step Into** menu option.

Sometimes you wish to step over procedures; you can do this by pressing **Shift+F8** or by choosing the **Debug | Step Over** menu option.

If you want to leave the procedure that you are currently stepping through and return to the line after which the procedure was called, press **Shift+Ctrl+F8**.

A useful feature is the **Run to Cursor** option from the debug speed menu, which allows you to execute code from the present position to the cursor. You activate this feature by pressing **Ctrl+F8**.

Watchpoints

It can be very tedious stepping through a long application, particularly if you know that the first one hundred times a loop is executed the correct result is produced and your breakpoint is hit every time it goes around that loop. Watchpoints are a type of breakpoint which will only cause the application to enter break mode when a specified condition is met.

To add a watchpoint, select the **Debug | Add Watch** menu option. The Add Watch window is displayed as shown in fig 11.7.

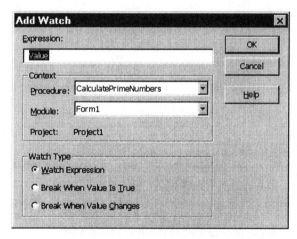

Fig 11.7 The Add Watch window.

There are three different types of watch which can be set:

- Continual display of a variable.
- Break only when a specified value is **True.**
- Break when a value changes.

In fig 11.8 the variable *Value* is shown, along with details of its type and scope.

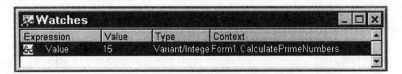

Fig 11.8 The Watch window.

Watchpoints can cause breaks when a specified value is **True** as shown in fig 11.9. Note that all the current watchpoints are displayed. In this figure, the value of the identifier *total* is out of context and so an appropriate message is displayed.

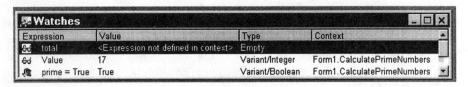

*Fig 11.9 Breaking when a value is **True**.*

The final useful variation of watchpoints is that a value can be specified which triggers a breakpoint only when it changes.

If you wish to change an existing watchpoint choose the **Debug | Edit Watch** menu option.

Conditional Compilation

Sometimes it is useful to put statements in your code which are there solely for debugging. When the application seems to be working correctly you could take these statements out, but if a problem is found later you may have to put many of these diagnostic statements back. Visual Basic offers an easy way around this. You can define a boolean variable, for example *DebugMode*, which you assign to **True** if you wish the debug statements to be compiled. If this variable is **False**, the code specified is not compiled and is therefore excluded from the application, as if you had deleted it. If a problem arises you can simply change this boolean to **True**.

To define the boolean constant:

> *#Const DebugMode = False*

The # before the reserved word **Const** indicates that this is a conditional compilation constant.

The conditionally compiled code is enclosed within a block:

> *#if DebugMode **Then***
>   *' Debugging code goes here*
>
>   ...
>
> *#Else*
>   *' Alternative non-debugging code goes here*

   ...

   #End if

The type of code that you might include when debugging are statements which display the values of variables, or visual indications that a particular point in the execution of the code has been reached.

The Call Stack window

A useful debug feature is the **View | Call Stack** menu option, which shows a list of the procedures called to reach the present breakpoint. The Call Stack window is shown in fig 11.10.

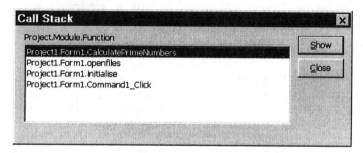

Fig 11.10 The Call Stack window.

In this example, the application is currently in the *CalculatePrimeNumbers* procedure, which was called from the *openfiles* procedure and so on.

The Debug menu

The **Debug** menu provides a shortcut way of using most common functions. To display this menu select the **View | Toolbars** menu and choose the **Debug** option. The **Debug** menu bar is shown in fig 11.11.

Fig 11.11 The Debug menu bar.

Some programmers prefer to use the shortcut keys while others prefer to use this menu, so choose the one you prefer and stick with it. Note that the first three icons on the **Debug** menu bar are duplicated on the standard menu bar.

Table 11.1 *The debug menu bar.*

Icon	Equivalent menu option	Description
	Run | Start	Starts the application running from the beginning.
	Run | Break	Breaks the currently running application.
	Run | Stop	Stops the currently running application.
	Debug | Toggle Breakpoint	Inserts a breakpoint at the current cursor position in the code window. If there is already a breakpoint it is removed.
	Debug | Step Into	Executes the next statement. If a procedure is called, the stepping continues through that called procedure.
	Debug | Step Over	Executes the next statement, but does not step into a procedure call.
	Debug | Step Out	Continues running the application, stopping at the line after which the current procedure was called.
	View | Locals Windows	Displays the Locals window.
	View | Immediate Window	Displays the Immediate window.
	View | Watch Window	Displays the Watch window.
	Debug | Quick Watch	Displays details of the current watch.
	View | Call Stack	Displays a list of every procedure that has been called to reach the current code position.

12
Object Oriented Programming

Introduction

Designing large applications is a complicated process and fraught with difficulties. While hardware always behaves in a predictable way the same is not true of software. All the applications we use have some sort of bugs in them. Even if an application was perfect it would be virtually impossible to prove it. In recent years there have been a number of design methodologies which provide a way of designing software to minimise the errors. The latest in this long list is object oriented design and programming.

In this chapter you will learn:

- What object orientation is.
- Why object orientation is important.
- How to use standard Visual Basic classes.
- How to define classes, methods and attributes.
- How to create and use objects.
- How to create and use collections.

Why use object oriented programming?

It is possible to program in Visual Basic without understanding or using its object oriented aspects, but in the longer term this will lead to problems since object orientation does make it easier to design software faster, with fewer bugs.

Microsoft have made it clear that they intend to adopt an increasingly object oriented approach to the design of their products. Microsoft have a huge market share and whatever they decide is the right direction often becomes an industry standard.

It is a sceptical viewpoint to state that we should switch to object orientation because Microsoft is moving in that direction, but in fact object orientation has been around for many years and has justifiably been growing in popularity. Object orientation provides a way of modelling real world objects which no other approach offers. It also allows software to be made up of reusable objects, which makes software writing faster and less error prone. Before we see how Visual Basic uses object orientation it is important to learn about the terminology and concepts of object oriented programming and design. Whether you are programming in Visual Basic, Delphi, C++, Java or any other modern development environment the concepts and jargon are the same.

What are objects?

Forms are objects as are the controls that we place on the form such as **CommandButton** and **Label** controls. Every object has its own data and code. The data includes the properties of the object, such as its colour and size, while the code includes the methods, such as **Show** and **Hide** which are two methods of **Form** class.

One of the key aspects of object oriented programming is that you can create a template or class which describes how an object which belongs to that class will behave. If you put a **CommandButton** on a form, you have created an object called *Command1*, which is a member of the **CommandButton** class.

Fig 12.1 Object classes and names.

Fig 12.1 shows the Properties window for this object. The Properties window shows only the design-time properties of the object, some properties are only available at run-time. In object oriented jargon, *Command1* is an instance of the **CommandButton** class. Since *Command1* is a member of the **CommandButton** class it has all the properties or attributes of that class. Every **CommandButton** has an **Appearance** property, a **BackColor** property and so on. Similarly every **CommandButton** has, for example, a **Click** method and a **DragDrop** method.

Every **CommandButton**, that is every instance of the **CommandButton** class, will have its own attribute values, for example, different values for the **Left** and **Top** properties which will give each button a different position on the form.

Every button can respond to a **Click** event, but there is a different **Click** event handler for each button. Buttons on a form are objects, while the button icon on the toolbox represents the **CommandButton** class.

The class defines the behaviour and properties. Objects are instances of a class and the way they behave is defined by the class they belong to. It is crucial to an understanding of object orientation to appreciate the difference between classes and objects.

Using properties

Visual Basic objects have properties, methods and events. In Visual Basic the data or attributes of an object are called the properties. The methods are procedures which can either change the value of a property or report on that value to another object. The events are actions which occur in your application which the object may respond to. You can use the following line of code to assign the **Text** property of a **TextBox** control called *Text1*:

*Text1.**Text** = "Why do memory prices change so much?"*

Text1 is the name of the object: it is an instance of the **TextBox** class. **Text** is a property of that object.

Similarly you can assign a variable to an object property as shown:

*ButtonWidth = Button1.**Width***

Using methods

In object oriented programming, methods are procedures that operate on the value of a property, for example:

*Form1.**Show***

This line of code displays an instance of the **Form** class called *Form1*, using the **Show** method.

Sometimes a method requires some information to be passed, for example:

*Form1.**Move** 50, 100, 500, 600*

This method sets the **Left, Top, Width, Height** properties of the object *Form1* to the specified values. When a method requires more than one parameter, as in this example, the parameters are separated by commas.

Creating objects at run-time

There are three ways of creating classes and objects in Visual Basic:

- Create a form and add controls to it at design time in the usual way as shown in fig 12.2.
- Create a class module, this is usually used for creating non-visual classes.
- Create an ActiveX control. This is one of the key features of this version of Visual Basic and is covered in chapter 13.

We are going to look first at how to create new instances of forms. You cannot create new controls by this method.

At run-time you can create a new instance of a form created at design time. If you create a form called *Form1*, which has a single button called *Command1* and add the following code to its click event:

```
Private Sub Command1_Click( )
Dim MyForm As New Form1
    MyForm.Top = Form1.Top + 200
    MyForm.Left = Form1.Left + 200
    MyForm.Show
End Sub
```

A new instance of the *Form1* object will be created as shown in fig 12.2.

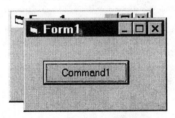

Fig 12.2 Creating new forms.

The new form appears slightly lower and to the right of *Form1* when it is displayed using the **Show** method. Note that it has its own button component.

The **New** keyword as shown in the previous example is a shorthand way of creating objects and is the style normally used, however you may see the same being achieved by using the **Set** keyword, which splits the declaration and the assigning of the object into two stages:

- Declare an object variable as a member of a class, in a similar way to declaring a normal variable, using the **Dim** statement.
- Assign the variable to the object using the **Set** statement.

For example:

> ***Dim*** *MyTextBox* ***As*** *TextBox1*
> ***Dim*** *BigForm* ***As New*** *Form1*

In these examples, *TextBox1* and *Form1* are existing objects created at design time. After declaring the object variable you have to assign it to an object before you can use it. This is done with the **Set** statement. The syntax for this statement is:

> ***Set*** *variable* = *object*

for example:

> ***Set*** *MyTextBox1*

To assign a **TextBox** called *MyTextBox* to another **TextBox** created at design time and to change its **Text** property, you can use this code:

> ***Dim*** *MyTextBox* ***As*** **TextBox**
> ***Set*** *MyTextBox* ***As*** *Text1*
> *MyTextBox.* ***Text*** = *"why are disks always nearly full?"*

The crucial things to note are that the object variable *MyTestBox* is declared as being a member of the **TextBox** class. In the **Set** statement *MyTextBox* can be assigned to any existing object of that type. In this case it is assigned to *Text1* (which is also a member of the **TextBox** class) and inherits all the property values of that text box, so it will be the same size, shape, colour and so on. You can change the value of the properties of the *MyTextBox* object, such as **Text**, in the same way as if it had been created at design time.

If you try this example, remember that because *MyTextBox* will have the same size and position as *Text1*, it will sit exactly on top of it unless you change its position.

Arrays of forms

If you are using many forms it is often useful to create an array of forms. The array is declared in a similar way to the declaration of variables:

> ***Dim*** *MyForm(10)* ***As New*** *Form1*

This statement creates an array of 11 (0→10) forms. If you amend the previous example so that the following code is executed on the button click event:

```
Private Sub Command1_Click( )
Dim MyForm(10) As New Form1
For c = 0 To 10
    MyForm(c).Top = Form1.Top + c * 100
    MyForm(c).Left = Form1.Left + c * 100
    MyForm(c).Show
Next c
End Sub
```

The forms shown in fig 13.2 are created.

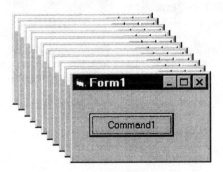

Fig 12.3 Creating new forms.

It would be extremely useful to be able to do a similar operation with controls. This can be achieved, but the technique is slightly different, since only forms are classes, the controls are not.

Arrays of control variables

You can create an array of controls, and add controls to and delete controls from it, but you can only create this control array at design time. Controls which are in an array have the same name, but you can distinguish between them by the **Index** property. When a control is not in an array, this property is null.

To create a control array, create the first control in the array and change its **Index** property to 0. Create a second control of the same type and change its name to be the same as the first. You will see the dialog box as shown in fig 12.3.

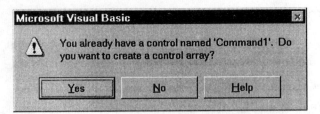

Fig 12.4 Creating a control array.

Click on *Yes*. The **Index** property is automatically assigned to 1. If you add a further control to the array, its **Index** property is assigned to 2. The application shown in fig 12.5 shows how this property has been used to indicate which of the three buttons in the control have been pressed and to display the result in a text box. The shared event procedure for this control array is:

```
Private Sub Command1_Click(Index As Integer)
    Text1.Text = "You have pressed button " + Str(Index)
End Sub
```

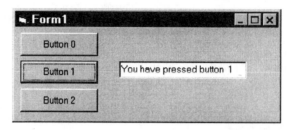

*Fig 12.5 Using the **Index** property.*

Although you cannot create a control array at run-time you can change the number of controls it contains. To add a control at run-time the **Load** method is used. Since the **Visible** property of a control which is added to a control array at run-time is always set to **False**, to add a control and display it you need the following lines of code:

```
Load Command1(Number)              'Number is the next free Index
Command1.Visible = True
```

The following example produces the form shown in fig 12.6. The control array is created at design time with a single button. The remainder are added at run-time. If you want to create a control array with only one control, you have to change the **Index** property from null to zero.

Fig 12.6 Adding controls at run-time.

The code for creating this form is shown below:

```
Private Sub Form_Load()
    XLimit = 3
    YLimit = 3
    For x = 0 To XLimit - 1
        For y = 0 To YLimit - 1
            Number = x * XLimit + y
            If Number <> 0 Then Load Command1(Number)
            Command1(Number).Top = y * Command1(0).Height
            Command1(Number).Left = x * Command1(0).Width
            Command1(Number).Caption = Str(Number)
```

> *Command1(Number).**Visible** = **True***
>   *Next y*
> *Next x*
> ***End Sub***

If you wish to delete an element of the array use the **Unload** method, for example:

> ***Unload** Command1(9)*

If you use **Unload** or **Load** more than once on a control array member you will generate a run-time error.

User-defined classes

Class modules can be used to create classes, these are usually non-visual. To add a class module to your project choose the **Project | Add Class Module** option.

The default name for a class module is *Class1*. To change the **Name** property, select the class module and view the Properties window, where you can change the **Name** property.

The next example is going to create a class called *Employee* which contains some data relating to individual employees and a method which is used for calculating the employees salary. The completed application is shown in fig 12.7.

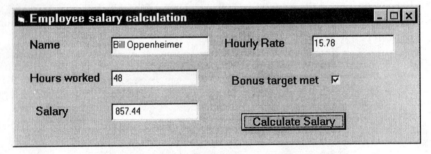

Fig 12.7 The user-defined Employee class.

To create this application:

- Create a new class module from the **Project | Add Class Module** menu option.
- Change the name of the class module to *Employee*. This is the name of the class.
- To add data to this class define the following identifiers in the general section of the module:

  Public** Name **As String
  Public** Hours **As Double
  Public** HourlyRate **As Double

> **Public** *Bonus* **As Double**
> **Public** *TargetMet* **As Boolean**

Next the method for this class has to be defined. This method calculates the salary by multiplying the hourly rate by the number of hours worked and adding a bonus if the targets have been met. It is typed after the identifier declaration:

> **Public Function** *Salary( )* **As Double**
>   *Salary = Hours * HourlyRate*
>   **If** *TargetMet* **Then** *Salary = Salary + Bonus*
> **End Function**

This has fully defined the *Employee* class, including all its data and its method. To test this class, the form shown in fig 12.7 is created. The default names of the **TextBox** controls are changed to *EmployeeName, HoursWorked, HourlyRate, TargetMet* and *EmployeeSalary.*

A new instance of the *Employee* class is created using the **Dim** statement:

> **Dim** *Bill* **As New** *Employee*

Each of the data elements of this object can be referenced using the following notation:

> *object.data*

For example, *Bill.Name* is the *Name* attribute (or property) of the object called *Bill.* In this example, the **Double** values of *Hours* and *HourlyRate* are specified as strings, which are converted to **Double** type using the **Val** function. Similarly when the salary has been calculated, it must be converted to a string using the **Str** function.

The *Salary* method is called using the same notation as for referring to object data, that is:

> *object.method*

for example, *Bill.Salary.* The complete listing of the click event for the button is shown below.

> **Private Sub** *Command1_Click( )*
>   **Dim** *Bill* **As New** *Employee*
>   *Bonus = 100#*
>   *Bill.Name = EmployeeName.***Text**
>   *Bill.Hours =* **Val***(HoursWorked.***Text***)*
>   *Bill.HourlyRate =* **Val***(HourlyRate.***Text***)*
>   *Bill.Bonus = Bonus*
>   **If** *Check1.***Value** *=* **Checked Then**
>   *Bill.TargetMet =* **True**
>   **Else:** *Bill.TargetMet =* **False**
>   **End If**
>   *EmployeeSalary.***Text** *=* **Str***(Bill.Salary)*
> **End Sub**

Creating and using Collections

Collections are an extremely useful way of grouping objects together. The objects do not need to be of the same type. To create an instance of the collection class use the **Dim** statement:

Dim *ControlCollection* **As New** *Collection*

This creates a collection called *ControlCollection*. Collections behave in a way which is similar to control arrays, but there are some important differences:

- Collections can have objects which are of different types.
- There are methods for adding and deleting members.
- **ReDim** is not needed to add or remove objects.
- Collections generally use less memory than arrays.

Every collection created has three new methods and one new property, in addition to the methods and properties they share, such as the **BackColor** property:

- The **Add** method adds a new object to the collection.
- The **Remove** method deletes an object.
- The **Item** method provides access to a member of the collection.
- The **Count** property is a read-only property which gives the number of objects in the collection.

In the next example, we are going to put **TextBox**, **Label**, **OptionButton** and **Frame** controls into a control array so that we can change the **BackColor** property which they share using the **Item** method. The completed application is shown in fig 12.8. When the button is clicked the **BackColor** of all the controls is changed.

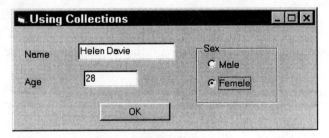

Fig 12.8 Using collections.

To add the first **TextBox** to the collection:

*ControlCollection.***Add** *Text1*

and so on for the other controls. The number of controls is given by the *Count* method, that is *ControlCollection.Count*.

The **Item** method followed by an index value allows the objects to be referenced, for example the third object is referred to as *Control.Collection.**Item**(3)*. The complete code for the **CommandButton** click event handler is shown below:

```
Private Sub Command1_Click( )
    Dim ControlCollection As New Collection
    ControlCollection.Add Text1
    ControlCollection.Add Text2
    ControlCollection.Add Option1
    ControlCollection.Add Option2
    ControlCollection.Add Label1
    ControlCollection.Add Label2
    ControlCollection.Add Frame1
    For c = 1 To ControlCollection.Count
        ControlCollection.Item(c).BackColor = RGB(220, 220, 220)
    Next c
End Sub
```

The **RGB** function is used to specify colours, it takes three parameters, the red, green and blue components of the colour. If you specify 0,0,0 this corresponds to black, while 255,255,255 corresponds to white.

13
ActiveX Controls

Introduction

ActiveX largely replaces custom controls and OLE (Object Linking and Embedding) in version 4. In version 4 of Visual Basic you could add OCX custom controls to your application, but you had to create them using an environment such as Visual C++. One of the key new features in version 5 is the ability to create new ActiveX controls. These controls are sometimes called custom controls.

In this chapter you will learn:

- What ActiveX controls are.
- How to create ActiveX controls.
- How to add your own properties to and events to an ActiveX control.
- How to use the ActiveX Control Interface Wizard.

What are custom controls?

ActiveX controls are user created controls, they have replaced the 32-bit OCX controls introduced in version 4 and the 16-bit VBX controls used in earlier versions.

When you have created your ActiveX control it can be used by any Visual Basic application that you create in exactly the same way as any of the standard Visual Basic controls. ActiveX controls can also be used in other development environments such as Delphi and Visual C++. Some web browsers such as Microsoft Explorer also provide support for ActiveX technology. ActiveX controls will not work with software which is pre-Windows 97 compatible.

The 16-bit VBX controls are no longer supported.

Creating an ActiveX control

The creation of the ActiveX control is superficially very straightforward, but if you want to create a control which is sufficiently complex to be useful and has an appropriate set of events and properties associated with it, there is a great deal of extra work to do. We are going to look at each of these steps in turn in order to create few custom controls.

To create an ActiveX control:

- Start a new application.
- You will be prompted to save your existing application.
- You will be asked to specify the type of project you want to start as shown in fig 13.1.
- Choose the **ActiveX Control** option.

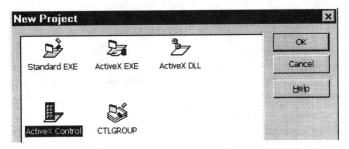

Fig 13.1 Creating an ActiveX control.

After the control has been created, you will need to start another project, and test the functionality of the control using that project. A shortcut way of doing this is to choose the **CTRLGROUP** option, which creates two projects, one is used creating the ActiveX control and the other for testing it. This alternative method is covered later in this chapter.

The ActiveX control we are going to create is a working analogue clock. The working control is shown in fig 13.2.

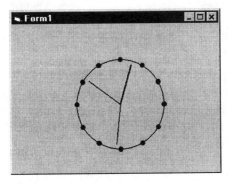

Fig 13.2 The completed ActiveX control.

The ActiveX clock

This ActiveX control, like most of the other controls you will make, consists of existing standard Visual Basic controls and methods. In this case a **Timer** control and three **Line** controls are used. The three lines are used to represent the hands of the clock. To create the ActiveX control:

- Click on the toolbox to select the **Timer** control.
- Position the **Timer** control anywhere on the design form.
- With the **Ctrl** button pressed, select the **Line** control and position this control anywhere on the form.
- Since you pressed the **Ctrl** button when selecting the **Line** control you do not need to select it again in order to place the other two **Line** controls on the form.

This application is unusual in that it does not matter what it looks like at design-time, since at run-time, the **Timer** control is invisible and the positions of the **Line** controls are changed every second as the clocks hands move.

The **Timer** control is by default not enabled, and the **Interval** property is zero. Set the **Enable** property to **True** and the **Interval** property to 1000. This will ensure that every 1000 milliseconds (that is every 1 second) a **Timer** event will occur.

If you are working with a number of controls of the same type and you want to perform similar action on them it is often useful to put them into a control array. Controls have the same name but are distinguished by the **Index** property. To put the three **Line** controls into a control array:

- Select the first **Line**, which will have a default name of *Line1*.
- Display the Properties box, and change its name property to *hand*.
- Change the **Index** property to 0, the first item in the control array.
- Change the **Visible** property to **False**. This will ensure that when the control is activated it does not initially display these lines.
- Since this line is to represent the hours hand which is normally thicker than the other hands, set the **BorderWidth** property to 2.
- Display the properties of the second **Line** control, by either selecting that control and then re-selecting the Properties window, or more efficiently by clicking on the right down arrow at the top of the Properties window, as shown in fig 13.3. The second line will have a default name of *Line2*, change this to *hand*.
- Next, change the name of the third **Line** control to *hand*.

When you change the **Name** property of the second **Line** control, the **Index** property will automatically change to 1. Similarly for the third **Line** control, called *Line2*, the **Index** property will be set to 2. Remember to set the **Visible** property of these two controls to **False**.

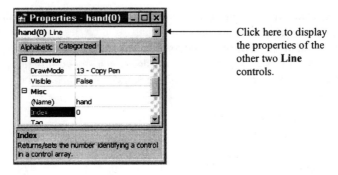

Click here to display
the properties of the
other two **Line**
controls.

*Fig 13.3 Putting the **Line** controls into a control array.*

At run-time you can address each of the elements of the control array by specifying its **Index**, for example to make the second line, which has an **Index** value of 1, visible, you can use the code:

hand(1).Visible = True

The advantage of using a control array is that if you had a large number of controls in the array you could make them all invisible by using a simple loop:

For *c=0* **To** *999*
  *myLine(c).Visible = **False***
Next *c*

The alternative is to assign each one separately, which would take a thousand lines of code.

If you want to use a different icon from the standard used for ActiveX controls, change the **ToolboxBitmap** property of the control to the bitmap you want to use.

Writing the code

Four variables need to be available throughout the form. These variables need to be declared:

***Private** seconds, minutes, hours, first*

The variables *seconds*, *minutes* and *hours* are used to save the value of each of these items. The identifier *first* is a **Boolean** variable which is assigned to **True** when the control is activated, so that the clock face can be drawn.

Three constants are also defined:

***Private Const** x = 1500, y = 1500, radius = 1000*

The variables *x* and *y* give the centre of the clock face, and also therefore one end of the clock hands. The *radius* variable gives the size of the clock face.

The first time the **Timer** event occurs, the face of the clock must be drawn. The position of the hours on the face are drawn as small solid circles. The **Boolean** *first* is tested and if it is **True** the *initialise* procedure is called.

The **X1**, **Y1** and **X2**, **Y2** properties of lines determine the co-ordinates of the two ends. In the initialise procedure, one end of the lines is assigned to the centre of the circle:

```
For c = 0 To 2
    hand(c).X1 = x
    hand(c).Y1 = y
Next c
```

The face of the clock is drawn using the **Circle** method:

```
Circle(x, y), radius
```

The small solid circles are drawn at 30 degree intervals around the clock face. The **FillStyle** property of the form they are drawn on is assigned to **vbFSSolid**, the default value of this property is **vbFSTransparent**. After drawing these circles, **FillStyle** must be assigned to **vbFSTransparent** again. One important thing to remember is that the **Cos** and **Sin** functions expect to receive an angle in radians not degrees. There are 2π radians in 360 degrees.

```
FillStyle = vbFSSolid
For c = 0 To 360 Step 30
    angle = c * (2 * 3.142 / 360)
    X1 = (radius * Cos(angle)) + x
    Y1 = (radius * Sin(angle)) + y
    Circle (X1, Y1), radius / 20
Next c
FillStyle = vbFSTransparent
```

Finally in this procedure the first variable is assigned to **False**, to ensure that this procedure is not called every time a **Timer** event occurs.

Whenever the **Timer** event occurs, the hands of the clock must be redrawn in their new position. The **Timer** function is called, this gives the number of elapsed seconds since midnight. The numbers of hours, minutes and seconds are given by:

```
hours = Timer / (60 * 60)
minutes = Fix((Timer / 60 - Fix(hours) * 60))
seconds = Fix(Timer - (Fix(hours) * 60 * 60 + (Fix(minutes) * 60)))
```

The **Fix** function returns the integer part of the number.

The co-ordinate system of the form is shown in fig 13.4. One end of all the hands is fixed at the centre of the clock face. This is the **X1** and **Y1** properties of the lines The position of the other hands is given by the **X2** and **Y2** properties:

```
X2 = radius * cos(angle)
Y2 = radius * sin(angle)
```

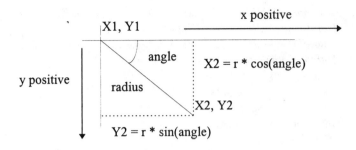

Fig 13.4 The co-ordinate system for the form.

The co-ordinate system for the form is different from that which is conventionally used, since the y axis is positive, moving vertically down the form rather than up. This can be taken into account by subtracting 90 degrees ($\pi/2$ radians) from the X2 and Y2 values:

*X2 = radius * cos(angle - π/2)*
*Y2 = radius *sin(angle - π/2)*

The code for doing this is:

```
' calculate the position of the hours hand
    angle(0) = hours * (360 / 12) * 2 * (3.142 / 360) - 2 * 3.142 / 4
' calculate the position of the minutes hand
    angle(1) = minutes * (360 / 60) * 2 * (3.142 / 360) - 2 * 3.142 / 4
' calculate the position of the seconds hand
    angle(2) = seconds * (360 / 60) * 2 * (3.142 / 360) - 2 * 3.142 / 4
```

Finally the hands must be drawn in their new position:

```
For c = 0 To 2
    hand(c).X2 = (radius * 0.9 * Cos(angle(c))) + x
    hand(c).Y2 = (radius * 0.9 * Sin(angle(c))) + y
    hand(c).Visible = True
Next c
```

The complete listing of the application is shown below:

```
Private seconds, minutes, hours, first
' x and y give the centre of the clock face
Private Const x = 1500, y = 1500, radius = 1000

Private Sub Timer1_Timer( )
    Dim angle(3)
    first = True
    If first = True Then initialise
    hours = Timer / (60 * 60)
    minutes = Fix((Timer / 60 - Fix(hours) * 60))
```

```
      seconds = Fix(Timer - (Fix(hours) * 60 * 60 + (Fix(minutes) * 60)))
' calculate the position of the hours hand
      angle(0) = hours * (360 / 12) * 2 * (3.142 / 360) - 2 * 3.142 / 4
' calculate the position of the minutes hand
      angle(1) = minutes * (360 / 60) * 2 * (3.142 / 360) - 2 * 3.142 / 4
' calculate the position of the seconds hand
      angle(2) = seconds * (360 / 60) * 2 * (3.142 / 360) - 2 * 3.142 / 4
' draw the hands
      For c = 0 To 2
            hand(c).X2 = (radius * 0.9 * Cos(angle(c))) + x
            hand(c).Y2 = (radius * 0.9 * Sin(angle(c))) + y
            hand(c).Visible = True
      Next c
End Sub

Private Sub initialise( )
      For c = 0 To 2
            hand(c).X1 = x
            hand(c).Y1 = y
      Next c
'Draw the face of the clock
      Circle (x, y), radius
'Draw the hour markings as filled circles
      FillStyle = vbFSSolid
      For c = 0 To 360 Step 30
            angle = c * (2 * 3.142 / 360)
            X1 = (radius * Cos(angle)) + x
            Y1 = (radius * Sin(angle)) + y
            Circle (X1, Y1), radius / 20
      Next c
      FillStyle = vbFSTransparent
      first = False
End Sub
```

Testing the control

If you want to test your control you cannot just click on the run icon, since custom controls can only work within another application. One of the new features of Visual Basic version 5 is that it allows you to have more than one project open at a time. This feature is used to open another project which provides an environment for the new control to run in.

To open another project:

- Select the **File | Save Project As** option.

- When prompted save the form name as *Clock* and the project name as *ActiveXClock*.
- Select the **File | Add Project** option.
- Choose the **Standard EXE** project type.
- Display the Project Explorer window by selecting the **View | Project Explorer** or using the icon on the toolbar.
- Change the name of the form in the new project to *TestingClock* and give it a suitable caption.
- Select the **File | Save Project Group As** option.
- When prompted save the form name as *TestingClock* and the project group name as *TestingClockProjectGroup*.

The Project Explorer will look like the one shown in fig 13.5.

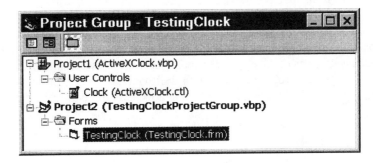

Fig 13.5 *The Project Explorer showing a project group.*

The project group consists of two projects, an **ActiveX Control** project and a **Standard EXE** project. You should keep the Project Explorer window visible since you will need to switch between the ActiveX control and the test project. To test your control close the design window for the ActiveX project and you will see that a new icon has been added to the toolbox as shown in fig 13.6. You can add your control to the form on the Standard EXE project in the same way as any other control.

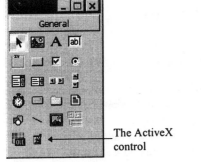

Fig 13.6 *The toolbox with the ActiveX control.*

The ActiveX control

If you do not close the design window of the ActiveX control, the ActiveX control icon in the toolbox will be greyed indicating that it is not available. If you do attempt to use it, you will receive the error message as shown in fig 13.7 This is a very common error.

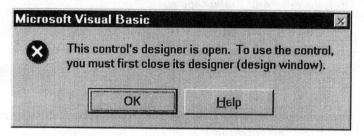

Fig 13.7 Resizing the ActiveX control.

To solve this problem close the design window for the **ActiveX Control** project and return to the **Standard EXE** project.

The control which we have created is useful, but it has a number of important limitations. The most obvious is that the clock does not resize when the frame it is inside is changed. Parts of the clock are simply obscured. A second limitation with this example is that this control does not have to deal with any events, or interact with the user. In the next section we are going to look at how these limitations are overcome.

Resizing Controls

One of the problems to be addressed with designing custom controls is that you need to be able to resize the controls. The first stage of dealing with the resizing of controls is to ensure that all the dimensions of the control are sized in terms of the dimension of the frame of the user control. The size of the control is given by the **Height** and **Width** properties. The control properties that we need to adjust when the control is re-sized are the centre position of the clock and its radius. These values are represented by x, y and *radius*, which are currently defined as constants. This needs to be changed by replacing the lines:

> ***Private*** *seconds, minutes, hours, first*
> ***Private Const*** *x = 1500, y = 1500, radius = 1000*

with the line:

> ***Private*** *seconds, minutes, hours, first, x, y, radius*

The identifiers x, y and *radius* need to be variables rather than constants.

When the control is resized the **Resize** event occurs. In this event, the values of x, y and *radius* can be altered to reflect the new size of the control. In addition the clock face and the hour marks will need to be withdrawn, so the variable *first* is assigned to **True**, so that the *initialise* procedure which draws the face and hour marks is called the next time the **Timer** event occurs. The **Resize** event is shown below:

```
Private Sub UserControl_Resize( )
    x = Width / 2
    y = Height / 2
    If (x > y) Then radius = 0.9 * y Else radius = 0.9 * x
    first = True
End Sub
```

The factor of 0.9 is used to provide some blank space around the clock to improve its appearance. The control may not be in a square container, therefore the smaller of the **Width** and **Height** properties are used to determine the radius.

An example of using the new resizable control at design time when producing a standard Windows EXE application is shown in fig 13.8.

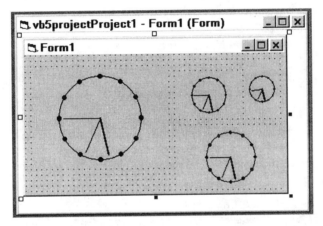

Fig 13.8 Resizing the ActiveX control.

Incorporating events in a Control

The clock control we have created is an unusual control since it has no associated event handlers. In this section we are going to look at how event handling can be incorporated into a custom ActiveX control.

When an application is accepting input, it is often essential to test the value which the user inputs. One of the most common tests is to ensure that a value which is typed is an integer. If it is not, an error message should be displayed. It is straightforward to do this sort of checking in Visual Basic, but if you are writing many applications it is tedious to have to duplicate the same code and is a possible source of errors. The ActiveX control we are going to create is a **TextBox** which will only accept an integer input:

- Start a new ActiveX project.
- Add a single **TextBox** control to the form.

- Declare the names of the two events we are creating in the general declarations section at the top of the code window for the form:

Public Event *NotaNumber( )*
Public Event *NotanInteger( )*

Different error messages will be displayed depending on whether the user inputs a non-numeric or a "." character.

When the text in the **TextBox** changes, the **KeyPress** event occurs. This event is used to determine if the "." character has been input. If it has, the **TextBox** is cleared and the input character which is passed to this event handler is changed to a null. This event handler is shown below:

```
Private Sub Text1_KeyPress(KeyAscii As Integer)
    If KeyAscii = Asc(".") Then
        RaiseEvent NotanInteger
        Text1.Text = ""
        KeyAscii = 0
    End If
End Sub
```

If an error is detected, the *NotanInteger* event occurs, due to the **RaiseEvent** statement.

Similarly code is added to the **Change** event handler for the **TextBox**, to see if a non-numeric character is input. If it is, a *NotaNumber* event is raised.

```
Private Sub Text1_Change( )
    If Not IsNumeric(Text1.Text) And Text1.Text <> "" Then
        RaiseEvent NotaNumber
        Text1.Text = ""
    End If
End Sub
```

This completes the basics of the new control. It must now be tested within the environment of the standard EXE project:

- Add the ActiveX control to the form
- Give the control a meaningful name, such as *IntegerTextBox*.
- Double click on the ActiveX control to go to the code window.
- Click on the left drop down list box at the top of the code window which displays the available controls in the project and select the *IntegerTextBox*.
- Click on the right drop down list to see the available events. The *NotanInteger* and the *NotaNumber* events are listed as shown in fig 13.9.

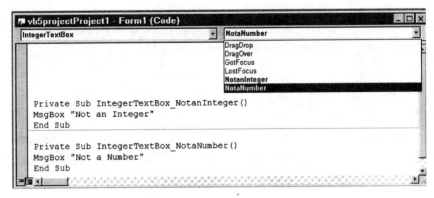

Fig 13.9 Adding the code for the custom events.

The code for these events displays a message box when an invalid input is detected. The code is shown below:

> ***Private Sub*** *IntegerTextBox_NotanInteger( )*
>   ***MsgBox*** *"Not an Integer"*
> ***End Sub***

> ***Private Sub*** *IntegerTextBox_NotaNumber( )*
>   ***MsgBox*** *"Not a Number"*
> ***End Sub***

If you create more than one instance of the custom control, event procedures are needed for each, in the same way, for example, that different buttons have different event handlers.

The final stage is to ensure that the control can resize and does not have any unnecessary blank space surrounding it. The code required is put into the **Resize** event:

> ***Private Sub*** *UserControl_**Resize**( )*
>   *Text1.**Width** = **Width***
>   *Text1.**Height** = **Height***
> ***End Sub***

The running test application with different sized custom **TextBox** controls and an error message after a non-numeric character has been typed into the top left **TextBox** is shown in fig 13.10.

The control we have created is functional, but it does not have all of the properties of a standard **TextBox**, for example you cannot change the size of type of the font. Next you will see how you add your own properties to a custom control and how to use the ActiveX wizards.

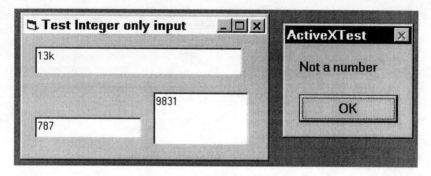

Fig 13.10 Resizing the custom control.

Making an OCX file

When the control is working satisfactorily you can create an OCX file which contains your control. It can then be used in other applications or distributed:

- Select the **File | Save Project As** menu option.
- Save the project as *ActiveXClock*.
- Select the **File | Make ActiveXClock.ocx** menu option.
- If you have created a previous version of this control, a warning dialog will be displayed, advising that you will overwrite the old version.
- Select the **File | New Project** menu option and create a **Standard EXE**.
- The ActiveX control that you have created must be added to the toolbar of this project.
- Select the **Project | Components** menu option. The dialog as shown in fig 13.11 will be displayed.

If you have saved your OCX file in the default folder, usually *c:windows\system* it will automatically be displayed in the list. If you have saved it in another folder, click the **Browse** button.

Click on the check box for your ActiveX control and then on the **OK** button. The toolbox will now contain your new control as shown in fig 13.6.

To include the ActiveX control in your application, simply click on it and then place it on your design form. If you have correctly created the control you will see the control appear on the form. It will be functioning with the hands moving even in the design mode of this application.

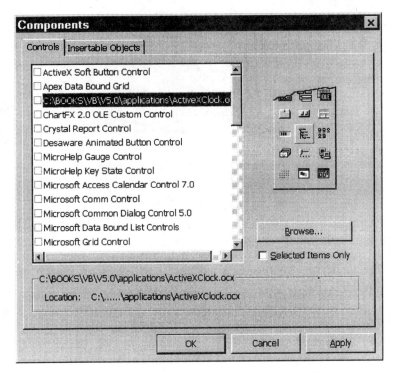

Fig 13.11 Adding an ActiveX control to the toolbar.

Control Groups

An alternative way to create an ActiveX control and an associated Standard EXE project is to select the **CTRLGROUP** option from the **File | New Project** menu. This creates an **ActiveX EXE** project and a **Standard EXE** project within a single project group.

The ActiveX Control Interface Wizard

In the next application we are going to use the **CTRLGROUP Project** option and the ActiveX Control Interface Wizard for creating an ActiveX control and adding our own properties to it. The application is not a very useful one in practical terms, but designing ActiveX controls is a difficult operation and the detail of how to do this is obscured if the control is a complex one which requires a lot of Visual Basic code to be written.

The working application is shown below in fig 13.12.

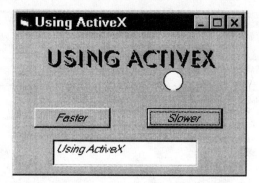

Fig 13.12 The complete application.

The ball bounces from side to side underneath the caption. The speed of the ball is determined by the two **CommandButton** controls, and the caption text by whatever is typed into the **TextBox**. The bouncing ball and the caption are a part of the ActiveX control. The buttons and **TextBox** are a part of the container application.

- To start the new project select the **File | New Project** menu option.
- Select the **CTRLGROUP** option from the displayed alternatives.
- If the Project Explorer window is not displayed, select the **View | Project Explorer** menu option.
- The Project Explorer is shown in fig 13.13.

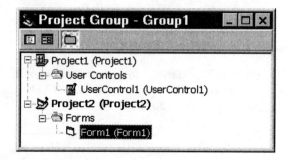

Fig 13.13 The Project Explorer.

The next stage is to design the visible parts of the ActiveX control:

- Using the Project Explorer switch the focus to the *UserControl1* form.
- Add a **Timer** control to the form.
- Change the **Interval** property to 100.
- Make sure that the **Enabled** property is **True** (this is the default).
- Add a **Shape** control to the form.
- Change the **Shape** property of the **Shape** control to **Circle**.
- Change the **BackStyle** property of the **Shape** control to **Opaque**.

The caption that the new control displays is a new property that we are going to add to the ActiveX control using the Control Interface Wizard.

The code to make the ball bounce from side to side must be added in the **Timer** event, which occurs whenever the **Timer** expires. The period between these events is determined by the **Timer** control **Interval** property. The code is shown below:

```
Private Change As Integer

Private Sub UserControl_Initialize( )
    Change = 50
    Shape1.Width = 300
    Shape1.Height = 300
    Shape1.Top = 400
    Shape1.Left = 0
End Sub

Private Sub Timer1_Timer( )
    Shape1.Left = Shape1.Left + Change
    If Shape1.Left + Shape1.Width > Width Then
        Shape1.Left = Width - Shape1.Width
        Change = -Change
    End If
    If Shape1.Left < 0 Then
        Shape1.Left = 0
        Change = -Change
    End If
End Sub
```

The first line declaring the identifier *Change* is in the general declarations section. This identifier controls how much the ball will move every time the **Timer** event occurs.

The *UserControl_Initialize* procedure establishes the initial size and position of the bouncing ball.

The *Timer1_Timer* event procedure controls the movement of the ball.

If you close the design window for the ActiveX control and switch the focus to *Project2*, you will see an icon representing the new control of the toolbar. Add a copy of this control to the form and you will see the ball moving from side to side. If you look at the Properties window for this control you will see many useful properties that you might like to use are not listed. The **Interval** and **Enabled** properties of the **Timer** and the **Shape** and **BackColor** properties of the **Shape** control are among those not listed. The next stage is to use the Control Interface Wizard to add these properties and a custom property which is used to display text.

Running the Control Interface Wizard

To run the ActiveX Control Interface Wizard select the **Add-Ins | ActiveX Control Interface Wizard**. If the Wizard is not listed on this menu you need to add it to your development environment using the **Add-Ins | Add-Ins Manager** menu option.

When you run the Wizard, a welcome screen is displayed first, followed by the window shown in fig 13.14.

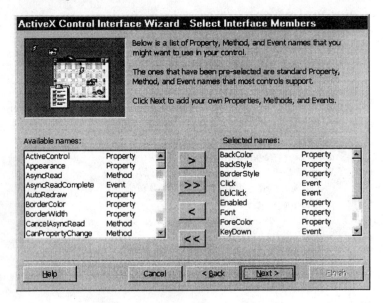

Fig 13.14 Selecting interface members.

This window allows you to select the properties, methods and event names that you want in your ActiveX control.

- The **Available names** list gives all of the available properties methods and events.
- The **Selected names** list gives all of the properties, methods and events which are currently to be included in your control.
- The keys with the single arrows on move selected items from one list to the other.
- The keys with the double arrows on move all the listed items.

The properties and events that we want to have available for our new control are the **Enabled** and **Interval** properties and the **Timer** event of the **Timer** control and the **Shape** and **BackColor** properties of the **Shape** control.

The **Enabled** and **BackColor** properties are already listed in the **Selected names** column. Add the **Shape** and **Interval** properties and the **Timer** event by selecting each item in the **Available names** list in turn and clicking on the single right pointing arrow.

Some of the properties and events listed in the *selected names* list are not required, for example, **MouseDown**, **MouseMove**, **MouseUp**, **KeyDown**, **KeyPress**, and **KeyUp**. These can be removed from the right list by selecting them and pressing the single left pointing arrow.

Click on the **Next** button to see the **Create Custom Interface Members** window as shown in fig 13.15.

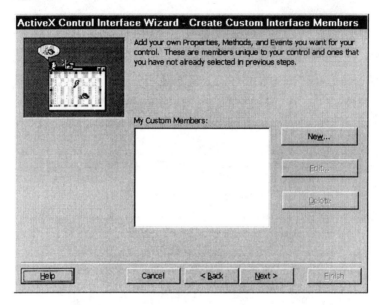

Fig 13.15 Creating custom interface members.

To add the property which displays the text at the top of the control click on the **New** button, to show the window displayed in fig 13.16:

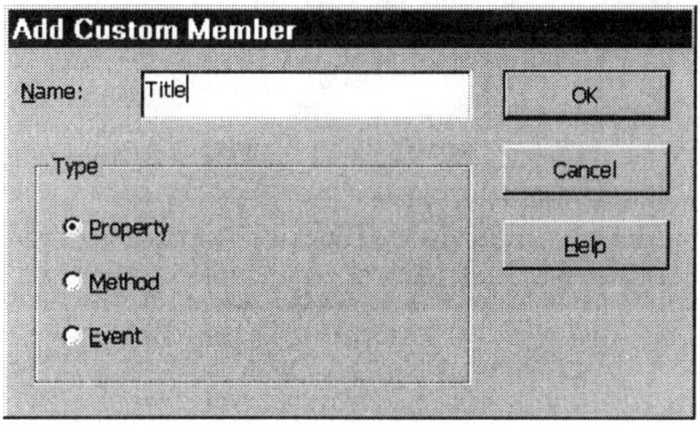

Fig 13.16 Adding custom members.

Give the new property the name of *Title* and press **OK**. Click on the **Next** button on the **Create Custom Interface** window to move to the **Set Mapping** window.

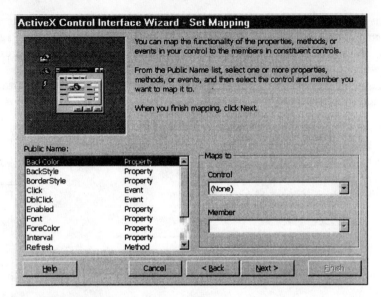

Fig 13.17 Mapping properties and events to controls.

The purpose of this window is to map the available properties, methods and events to controls within the custom control or to the whole control, for example the **Enabled** property could be mapped to the whole control or just to the **Timer** control. The **BackColor** property could be mapped onto the **Shape** control, or to the whole ActiveX control.

Most of the properties, events and methods are to be mapped onto the whole ActiveX control:

- Select all the controls in the list by pressing the **Shift+End** keys.
- Deselect the **BackColor**, **Enabled**, **Interval**, **Shape** and **Title** properties and the **Timer** event by holding the **Ctrl** key and clicking on each of the items in turn.
- In the **Control** box, select *UserControl*.
- Select the **Timer** event by clicking on it.
- Press **Ctrl** and click on the **Enabled**, and **Interval** properties to select them.
- In the **Control** box, select *Timer1*.
- Select the **Shape** property.
- In the **Control** box select *Shape1*.

The last remaining property to be mapped is the *Title* property which we have created. To do this click on the **Next** button to display the window shown in fig 13.18.

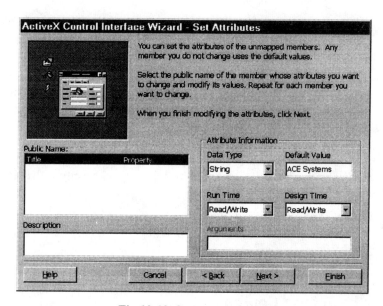

Fig 13.18 Setting attributes.

Change the **Data Type** to **String** and the **Default Value** to *ACE Systems*. All the other attributes remain unchanged.

Click on the **Next** button to display a finished screen which gives you the option of seeing a summary report, which contains some useful information on how to test your control.

If you look at your code modules for the ActiveX control you will see that the Wizard has added a vast amount of code which is required to make the events, properties and methods you have specified, available to the designer who uses this control. You will notice that the code is littered with comments and strong warnings:

WARNING DO NOT REMOVE OR MODIFY THE FOLLOWING COMMENTED LINE.

This is a warning which should be taken very seriously. In theory there is no limit to the number of times that you can run the Wizard if you want to change your interface, in practice some users have reported problems occurring through repeated use of the Wizard, so it is advisable to design your application thoroughly and to use the Wizard the minimum number of times, ideally once only.

The control is now virtually complete, but needs some code before it will work correctly to display the text. The text needs to be displayed in a variety of positions in the code, for example, when the control is resized, so a small procedure has been written which can be called from these places:

- Select the **Tools | Add Procedure** option.
- Type the **Name** *DisplayTitle*.
- Specify the **Type** as **Sub.**
- Specify the **Scope** as **Private.**

Add the following text to this procedure.

```
Private Sub DisplayTitle( )
    UserControl.Cls
    UserControl.Print m_Title
End Sub
```

The **Cls** method clears all the text generated at run-time from a form. The **Print** method displays the specified text. The Wizard places the prefix *m_* in front of its variables, so the text we wish to display is *m_Title*.

The *DisplayTitle* procedure must be called anywhere an event occurs which will cause it to be redrawn. The most obvious place is in the **Resize** event. To add the **Resize** event select the **Tools | Add Procedure** option and specify a **Private Sub** as shown below:

```
Private Sub UserControl_Resize( )
    DisplayTitle
End Sub
```

Testing the ActiveX Control

If you close the design window of the new control and shift the focus to *Project2*, you will see the icon for the ActiveX control. Add this to the form, and you will see that the ball moves from side to side, but there is no text, however if you resize the control the text is displayed. If you change the size and font using the **Font** property, there is no change in the displayed text, until the control is resized. To overcome this limitation, calls to the *DisplayTitle* procedure must be made whenever there is an event which changes the text, for example whenever the font is changed.

```
Public Property Set Font(ByVal New_Font As Font)
    Set UserControl.Font = New_Font
' Add the following line to the procedure created by the Wizard
    DisplayTitle
    PropertyChanged "Font"
End Property
```

Similarly whenever the text is changed, the change is reflected immediately in the design screen.

```
Public Property Let Title(ByVal New_Title As String)
    m_Title = New_Title
' Add the following line to the procedure created by the Wizard
    DisplayTitle
    PropertyChanged "Title"
End Property
```

To ensure that the title is displayed whenever the control is refreshed, the procedure shown below must be modified to include the call to *DisplayTitle*.

```
Public Sub Refresh( )
    UserControl.Refresh
' Add the following line to the procedure created by the Wizard
    DisplayTitle
End Sub
```

Project2 with the ActiveX control at design time is shown in fig 13.19.

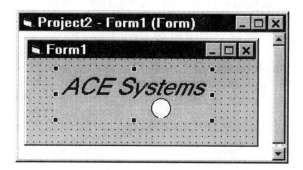

***Fig 13.19** Project2 with the ActiveX control at design time.*

The properties such as the colour of the ball (**BackColor**) and the text (**Title**) can be changed at design time and at run-time. To complete the application two buttons are added which make the ball move faster and slower and a **TextBox** is added.

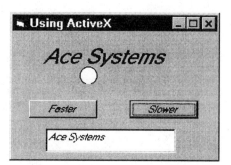

***Fig 13.20** The running application.*

As text is typed it appears as a caption. The two **CommandButton** controls determine the speed of the bouncing ball. The only code needed is in the change event for the **TextBox** and the click events for the buttons:

```
Private Sub Faster_Click( )
    UserControl11.Interval = UserControl11.Interval / 2
End Sub

Private Sub Slower_Click( )
    UserControl11.Interval = UserControl11.Interval * 2
End Sub
```

```
Private Sub Text1_Change( )
    UserControl11.Title = Text1.Text
End Sub
```

The buttons have been named *Faster* and *Slower*. One feature of this application is that the limitation on speed is how fast the screen can be updated, which is dependent on your computer. If the **Interval** between the **Timer** events is too small there is insufficient time to update the screen and the ball appears to stop.

This application could be refined to be more sophisticated, for example re-sizing itself as the size of the text changes. You have to write some Visual Basic code to do this as shown in earlier examples.

If you want other applications to use the control you need to produce the OCX file you need to save the application using the **File | Save Project Group As** option and then after giving the ActiveX project the focus select the **File | Make** option.

14

Creating and Using Menus

Introduction

Menus are a key feature of virtually all Windows programs. Fortunately Visual Basic provides a set of tools that allow you to define the menus that you want in an interactive way.

In this chapter you will learn how to:

- Create and amend menu bars.
- Use shortcut keys to invoke menu items.
- Disable and enable menu items.
- Create and use pop-up menus.

Creating a menu bar

To create a menu click on the menu editor icon on the toolbar as shown in fig 14.1, or select the **Tools | Menu Editor** menu option.

Fig 14.1 The Menu Editor icon.

The Menu Editor dialog box is displayed as shown in fig 14.2.

The **Caption** is the menu title item which appears on the menu bar, for example, *File*, or *Help*. As the caption is typed it appears in the large window at the bottom of the form.

The **Name** is used to reference the menu control bar from your code. Every control needs a name.

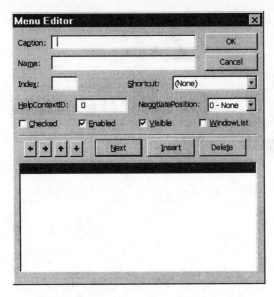

Fig 14.2 The Menu Editor.

To create the menu, type the **Caption** and **Name** for the first menu caption.

* Select **Next** to make another entry.
* Specify a new **Caption** and **Name**. If this control is a menu item, not a title item, press the right arrowed button on the form.
* A separator bar can be created by putting a hyphen as the **Caption**.

Fig 14.3 shows the completed Menu Editor window.

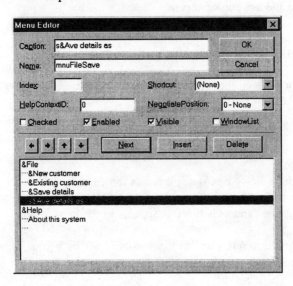

Fig 14.3 The completed menu.

Amending the menu

Visual Basic allows you to easily amend a menu:

- Open the Menu Editor.
- Select the entry in the menu that you want to change.
- Click on **Insert** to make another entry before the selected control.
- Click on **Delete** to remove the selected control.
- Move between the menu items by using the up and down arrow keys.
- Change the level of the menu item by using the left and right arrows.

When a menu item is selected a **Click** event occurs and Visual Basic constructs a template procedure for processing this event.

Shortcut keys

Visual Basic allows you to specify "shortcut" keys for invoking menu elements, as shown in fig 14.4, so that the elements can be selected from the keyboard as well as by the mouse.

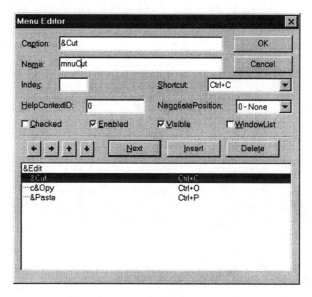

Fig 14.4 Specifying shortcut keys.

For a pull-down menu that appears on the menu bar, for example, **File** and **Help**, the menu can be opened by pressing **Alt** with the underlined character from the menu title, for example, **Alt+F** opens the **File** menu. The character of the menu title to be underlined is indicated by the "&" character in the **Caption** field on the **Menu Design** Window, for example, "**&File**".

For an element on a displayed menu, the element can be displayed by pressing the underlined character of the caption. As for the menu title, the character of a menu element to be underlined is indicated by the "&", for example, **E&xit** on the **File** menu can be invoked by keying that character ("x").

- Menu items can be invoked directly by setting the **ShortCut** list in the Menu Design window.
- The shortcut keys are displayed on the dropdown combo.

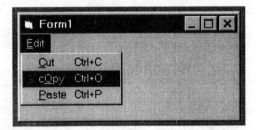

Fig 14.5 Shortcut keys.

You can have shortcut keys that invoke menu elements directly, even when they are not being displayed. These are set from the **Shortcut** combo in the menu editor dialog. Shortcut keys are displayed on the menu to the right of the corresponding element, for example, "*Cut* **Ctrl+X**".

The Checked property

Menu elements can have a check mark displayed alongside them by setting the **Checked** property:

Control_name.Checked = True

- The **WindowList** check box is used with an MDI application to indicate if the menu control displays a list of open child windows.
- The **HelpContextId** text box is used to assign a unique context identifier. This is used to find the Help topic in the Help file.

Enabling and disabling controls

Sometimes menu controls need to be disabled, for example, the **Paste** command in an editor if nothing has been **Cut** or **Copied** beforehand. All the menu commands have an **Enabled** check box. If this is set to **False** the menu control appears in light grey and does not respond to clicking. The run-time command is of the form:

Control_name.Enabled = False

- If a menu title is disabled all the controls below it are automatically disabled.

- Menu controls can also be disabled by making them invisible:

  Control_name.Visible = False

If there are other menu items on the title bar a gap is not left where the invisible menu item had been, the menu items on the right of the menu item shift left to fill the gap.

Pop-up Menus

Pop-up menus have become increasingly important for providing a set of context sensitive options. To display a pop-up menu you use the **PopupMenu** method, if the menu system shown in fig 14.6 is created using the Menu Editor.

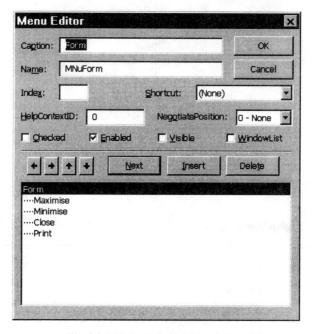

Fig 14.6 Creating a pop-up menu.

The *Form* menu item is called *MnuForm* and has four sub-items. Since this is to be a pop-up menu item its **Visible** property must be set to **False** when the form is loaded so that it is not displayed on the menu bar:

> *Private Sub Form_Load( )*
> *MnuForm.Visible = False*
> *End Sub*

If you want to add additional pop-up menus you can do so in the same way. If you want menu items to remain on the menu bar, leave their **Visible** property to the default value of **True**.

To display the form when the right mouse button is clicked the **MouseDown** event handler for the form must test to see if the right button has been clicked and then call the **PopupMenu** method:

> *Private **Sub** Form_MouseDown(Button **As Integer**, Shift **As Integer**,*
> *X **As Single**, Y **As Single**)*
>   *If Button = 2 **Then PopupMenu** MnuForm*
>   ***End Sub***

The pop-up menu displayed is shown in fig 14.7.

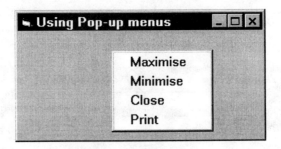

Fig 14.7 Displaying the pop-up menu.

In the example shown only the single mandatory parameter, the name of the menu, is given, but there are a further five optional parameters. The full syntax for this method is: .

> *object.PopupMenu menuname, flags, x, y, boldcommand*

*Table 14.1 The **PopupMenu** method.*

Parameter	Comments
object	Optional. If omitted, the menu applies to the form with the focus is the object.
menuname	Required. The name of the pop-up menu. The menu specified must have at least one sub-menu.
flags	Optional. A value which specifies the location and behaviour of the menu. This is described below in detail.
x	Optional. The x co-ordinate of the menu. If omitted the x mouse position is used.
y	Optional. The y co-ordinate of the menu. If omitted the y mouse position is used.
boldcommand	Optional. The name of a menu control to display in bold. If omitted none are bold.

The values for the flag parameter are in two parts which describe both the location and behaviour:

Table 14.2 *The location values for the flags parameter.*

Constant	Value	Description
vbPopupMenuLeftAlign	0	The left of the menu is at the x position.
vbPopupMenuCenterAlign	4	The centre is at x.
vbPopupMenuRightAlign	8	The right is at x.

Table 14.3 *The behaviour values for the flags parameter.*

Constant	Value	Description
vbPopupMenuLeftButton	0	The selected item on the menu reacts to the click of the left mouse button.
vbPopupMenuRightButton	2	The selected item reacts to the click of the right mouse button.

If optional parameter are omitted and a later parameter is to be specified, commas must be used to specify the missing parameter, for example in the code below the *flags* parameter is omitted.

> *Form1.MnuForm , , 200, 300*

To use the *flags* parameter it is clearer if you use the constants, for example:

> *Form1.MnuForm,* **vbPopupMenuLeftAlign** + **vbPopupMenuRightButton**, *50,200*

The x and y co-ordinates are relative to the position of the form which displays the menu.

15

Using Custom Controls

Introduction

In addition to the standard Visual Basic controls there are many custom or ActiveX controls. In this chapter we are going to see how custom controls are incorporated into your toolbox and how some of the most popular custom controls behave. In particular we are going to look in detail at the grid control which allows you to display and manipulate data in tables.

In this chapter you will learn about:

- Incorporating custom controls into your toolbox.
- The Common dialog control.
- Creating and using grids.

The CommonDialog control

Custom controls are installed by using the **Projects | Components** menu option. There are thousands of custom controls available from third parties as well as some supplied with Visual Basic 5. One of the most useful is **CommonDialog** control. To install it select *Microsoft Common Dialog Control V5.0* from the components dialog as shown in fig 15.1. The icon for this control, shown in fig 15.1, appears on the toolbox.

*Fig 15.1 The **CommonDialog** control.*

The **CommonDialog** control performs a variety of functions depending on which method is used.

Table 15.1 *The CommonDialog control.*

Description	Method
No action.	-
Displays **ColorDialogBox**	**ShowColor**
Displays **OpenDialogBox**	**ShowOpen**
Displays **SaveAsDialogBox**	**ShowSave**
Displays **FontDialogBox**	**ShowFont**
Displays **PrinterDialogBox**	**ShowPrinter**
Displays **HelpDialogBox**	**ShowHelp**

To display the Open dialog box use the command:

*CommandDialog1.**ShowOpen***

To use the common dialog control successfully, the Microsoft Windows dynamic link library *Commdlg.dll* must be in the *Windows/System* folder. The default name of the first common dialog box to be created is *CommonDialog1*.

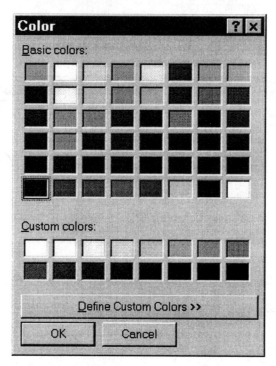

Fig 15.2 The Color dialog box.

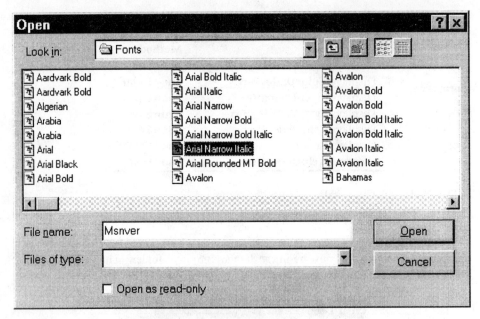

Fig 15.3 *The Open dialog box.*

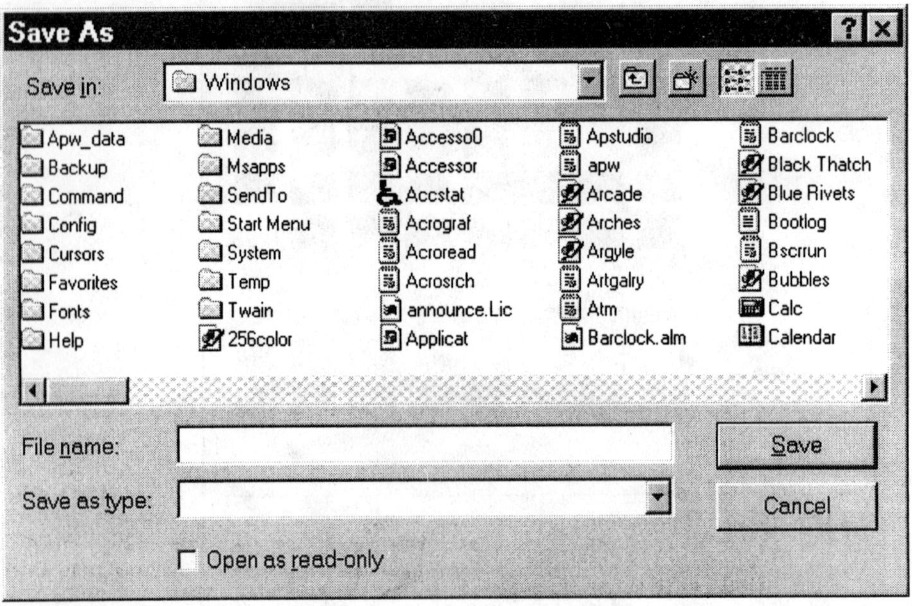

Fig 15.4 *The SaveAs dialog box.*

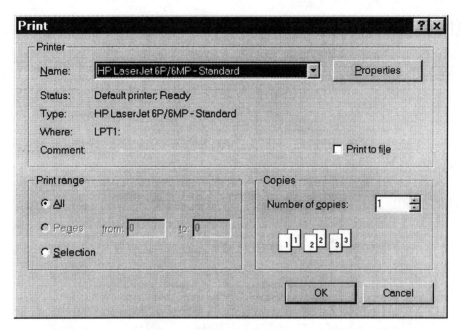

Fig 15.5 The Printer dialog box.

Windows 95 automatically provides the **What's this** help button. Click the right mouse button over any control of the dialog and a **What's this** button appears. Click on it, for help information.

Common Controls

Do not confuse the common dialog control with the *Microsoft Windows Common Controls V5.0 Controls.* If you choose this option you will find the following additional controls added to your toolbox:

- **TabStrip.**
- **Toolbar.**
- **StatusBar.**
- **ProgressBar.**
- **TreeView.**
- **ListView.**
- **ImageList.**
- **Slider.**

The Calendar control

To add this control to the toolbox, select the *Microsoft Access Calendar Control V7.0* from the **Projects | Components** menu.

*Fig 15.6 The **Calendar** control.*

The working calendar control is shown in fig 15.7. This control has a wide range of properties that you can change and events that you can respond to.

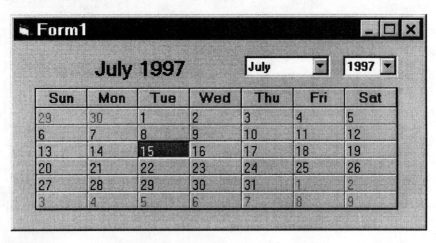

*Fig 15.7 The **Calendar** control at run-time.*

The Grid Control

One of the most useful of the custom controls is the **Grid** control. To add this choose the *Microsoft Grid Control* option from the **Project | Components** menu.

*Fig 15.8 The **Grid** control.*

After you have installed the **Grid** control it will now be displayed in the toolbox as shown in fig 15.8.

Grids allow you to display information in rows and columns.

- Each cell in the grid can be controlled separately.
- Rows can be added and deleted at run-time.
- Columns can be added and deleted at run-time.

Fig 15.9 shows an example of the **Grid** control at design time.

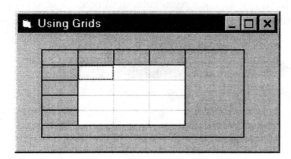

*Fig 15.9 The **Grid** control.*

Uses of the Grid control

Grid controls are useful if you want to display information in tables. An example of the type of information that you might want to display is shown in fig 15.10.

Name	Department	Age
Bill Simmons	Finance	57
Pam Smith	Graphic Design	32
Malcolm Yates	International Sales	38

Fig 15.10 Displaying tabular information.

Grid controls are very widely used, but are not as intuitive as most of the other controls, and it is worthwhile looking in more detail at their properties and methods.

Changing the number of rows and columns

Many of the properties of grids can only be controlled at run-time not at design time, including such basic properties as the number of rows and columns in the grid and the text that they contain. The most usual place to initialise these properties is in the **Load** event for the form. For example, to change the number of rows and columns in a grid use the **Rows** and **Cols** properties:

```
Private Sub Form_Load( )
    Grid1.Rows = 4
    Grid1.Cols = 3
End Sub
```

As a default there will be one fixed row and one fixed column of cells. These have a grey background and do not scroll. The code above produces the grid shown in fig 15.11.

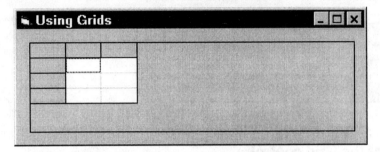

*Fig 15.11 The **Rows** and **Cols** properties.*

To change the number of fixed rows and columns use the **FixedCols** and **FixedRows** properties, for example:

> *Grid1.**FixedRows** = 0*

Changing grid text

The text in grid cells can only be changed at run-time. The **Text** property refers to the currently active cell, this is determined by the value of the **Row** and **Col** property, for example, to create the headings at the top of the columns:

```
Grid1.Col = 0
Grid1.Row = 0
Grid1.Text = "Name"
Grid1.Col = 1
Grid1.Text = "Department"
Grid1.Col = 2
Grid1.Text = "Age"
```

If you want to add a lot of text to a grid it can be very tedious doing it a cell at a time, if the data you want to store is put into an array the number of lines of code required is reduced. For example:

```
Names = Array("Bill Simmons", "Pam Smith", "Malcolm Yates")
Departments = Array("Finance", "Design", "International Sales")
Ages = Array("57", "32", "38")
For TheCol = 0 To 2
    Grid1.Col = TheCol
    For TheRow = 1 To 3
        Grid1.Row = TheRow
        If Grid1.Col = 0 Then Grid1.Text = Names(TheRow - 1)
```

> > *If Grid1.Col = 1 Then Grid1.Text = Departments(TheRow - 1)*
> > *If Grid1.Col = 2 Then Grid1.Text = Ages(TheRow - 1)*
> *Next TheRow*
> *Next TheCol*

Changing size

To change the size of a column or row use the **ColWidth** and the **RowWidth** properties.

> *Grid1.ColWidth(2) = 1800*

The value following **ColWidth** specifies the column you are referring to. Note that the first column is zero.

To change the overall size of the grid use the **Height** and **Width** properties, for example:

> *Grid1.Height = 3000*

The complete code to display the grid shown in fig 15.10 is given below:

```
Private Sub Form_Load( )
    Names = Array("Bill Simmons", "Pam Smith", "Malcolm Yates")
    Departments = Array("Finance", "Design", "International Sales")
    Ages = Array("57", "32", "38")

    Grid1.Rows = 4
    Grid1.Cols = 3
    Grid1.Col = 0
    Grid1.Row = 0
    Grid1.Text = "Name"
    Grid1.Col = 1
    Grid1.Text = "Department"
    Grid1.Col = 2
    Grid1.Text = "Age"
    Grid1.ColWidth(0) = 1800
    Grid1.ColWidth(1) = 2500
    Grid1.ColWidth(2) = 400
    Grid1.Width = 50
    For c = 0 To Grid1.Cols - 1
        Grid1.Width = Grid1.Width + Grid1.ColWidth(c)
    Next c
    Grid1.FixedCols = 0
    For TheCol = 0 To 2
        Grid1.Col = TheCol
        For TheRow = 1 To 3
```

```
            Grid1.Row = TheRow
            If Grid1.Col = 0 Then Grid1.Text = Names(TheRow - 1)
            If Grid1.Col = 1 Then Grid1.Text = Departments(TheRow - 1)
            If Grid1.Col = 2 Then Grid1.Text = Ages(TheRow - 1)
        Next TheRow
    Next TheCol
End Sub
```

Selecting cells

When a cell has been selected the **CellSelected** property is set to **True**, otherwise it is set to **False**. This property is only at run-time not design time, for example:

```
Grid1.CellSelected = True
```

Sometimes it is useful to select an area. The selected area is defined by four properties which specify the limits of the selected area. These properties are:

- **SelEndCol**.
- **SelStartCol**.
- **SelEndRow**.
- **SelStartRow**.

Many cells can be selected but only one cell can be active - this is the cell specified by the **Row** and **Col** properties. An active cell need not be selected. Selected cells are highlighted, while the active cell has a dotted border.

Adding and removing rows

You can add new rows at run-time using the **AddItem** method as shown below:

```
Private Sub Form_Load( )
    Grid1.Rows = 1
    Grid1.Cols = 3
    For c = 1 To 5
        Grid1.AddItem "Row" & c
    Next c
End Sub
```

The running application is shown in fig 15.12. Since all of the rows cannot be shown at the same time in the space available, a vertical scroll bar is automatically added.

As a default a new row is added after the existing rows, but you can insert a new row at any position in the grid, for example:

```
Grid1.AddItem "New Row" , 3
```

inserts a new row 3.

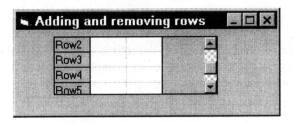

Fig 15.12 *Adding and removing rows.*

To specify the contents of more than one cell along a row, separate the cell contents by tabs, an easy way of specifying a tab is to use **Chr$(9)**:

*Grid1.**AddItem** "one"&Chr$(9) & "two" & Chr$(9) & "three"*

- You cannot use **AddItem** with fixed rows.
- The **AddItem** method actually creates a new row - it does not simply put text into an existing row.

You can also remove rows at run-time using:

*Grid.**RemoveItem** index*

- The value of *index* specifies the number of the row to be removed.
- You cannot use **RemoveItem** with fixed rows.

Aligning text

It is important that the text displayed in grids is correctly for a professional appearance. Text in cells can be aligned using the **ColAlignment** and the **FixedAlignment** properties.

- The **FixedAlignment** property specifies the type of alignment for fixed cells and **ColAlignment** for all other cells. For example:

*Grid1.**FixedAlignment**(0) = vbLeftJustify*
*Grid1.**ColAlignment**(2) = vbCenter*

Table 15.2 *The **Alignment** property.*

Value of Alignment	Meaning
vbLeftJustify	Left justified
vbRightJustify	Right justified
vbCenter	Centred

The default is left justified.

Scroll bars

If there is not enough room to display all the cells in a grid horizontal or vertical scroll bars are automatically added. However you can explicitly control whether scroll bars are displayed or not using the **ScrollBars** property, for example:

Grid1.ScrollBars = grdVertical

The possible values of the **ScrollBars** property are shown in table 15.3.

Table 15.3 The ScrollBars property.

Value of ScrollBars	Meaning
grdNone	No scroll bars.
grdHorizontal	Horizontal scroll bars.
grdVertical	Vertical scroll bars.
grdBoth	Horizontal and vertical scroll bars.

The default is for both horizontal and vertical scroll bars.

Editing grid cells

One limitation of the **Grid** control is that the user cannot directly edit the contents of a cell without some additional code being written. If you do want to offer this facility there is a standard way of doing it, but it is rather clumsy.

- Create a **TextBox** control and make it invisible, by setting the **Visible** property to **False**.
- When you click on a cell, the click event processing routine for the cell transfers the focus to the **TextBox**, makes it visible and positions it so that it fits exactly over the cell.
- It requires some tedious but straightforward arithmetic to make sure that the **TextBox** is exactly the same size as the grid cell.
- Most people write a subroutine to do this as it is a common operation if you are frequently working with grids.
- When you press **Return**, the contents of the **TextBox** are transferred to the grid cell and the **TextBox** is made invisible.

If you want to offer this facility it is advisable to use one of the many grid controls available from third party vendors which have this facility.

16
Creating and Using Graphics

Introduction

Good graphics can make the difference between an attractive easy-to-use application and one which is dull and awkward. Visual Basic provides an excellent set of tools for adding graphics at design and run-time.

In this chapter you will learn about:

- The **Line** and **Shape** controls.
- The **Image** and **PictureBox** controls.
- The Visual Basic co-ordinate system.
- How to create your own graphics.
- How to add graphics at design and run-time.

The graphics controls

Visual Basic has two controls for creating your own simple graphics which are made up of simple shapes such as lines, squares and circles:

- The **Line** control draws a straight line.
- The **Shape** control draws either a square, a circle, a rectangle, or an oval.

These controls are shown in fig 16.1.

There are two controls which act as containers for adding existing graphics to your application:

- The **Image** control, shown in fig 16.2.
- The **PictureBox** control, shown in fig 16.3.

Line control

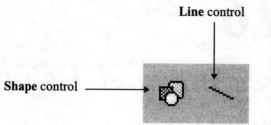

Fig 16.1 The Line and Shape controls.

Shape control

The **PictureBox** and **Image** controls have a very similar function, but there are subtle differences between them. They are covered later in this chapter.

Fig 16.2 The PictureBox control.

Fig 16.3 The Image control.

The Line control

To draw a line at design time:

• Select the **Line** control.
• Press the left mouse button at the start position of the line and drag.
• Release the mouse where you want to position the end of the line.

Table 16.1 Properties of the Line control.

Property	Description
BorderColor	The colour of the drawn line.
BorderStyle	The style of the line, for example dotted.
BorderWidth	The thickness of the line. 1 is the minimum. 8192 the maximum.
DrawMode	The colour of the line is dependent on **BorderColor** and also the colour being drawn on.
Name	The name of the control.
Visible	If set to **True** the line is displayed.
X1	The horizontal co-ordinates of the start of the line.
X2	The horizontal co-ordinates of the end of the line.
Y1	The vertical co-ordinates of the start of the line.
Y2	The vertical co-ordinates of the end of the line.

The most commonly used properties of the **Line** control are shown in table 16.1.

The **BorderStyle** property exists for many controls and can have three different meanings depending on which control it applies to, for example, for **Form** objects the property determines the border, while for **Line** objects this property determines the thickness of the line. There are seven possible constants which can be assigned to the property for the **Line** control as shown in table 16.2.

*Table 16.2 The **BorderStyle** property.*

Constant	Value	Description
vbTransparent	0	Transparent.
vbBSSolid	1	The line is unbroken. This the default.
vbBSDash	2	Dashed.
vbBSDot	3	Dotted.
vbBSDashDot	4	Dash - dot.
vbBSDashDotDot	5	Dash - dot - dot.
vbBSInsideSolid	6	An unbroken line.

In practical terms there is no difference between assigning a value of **vbBSSolid** and **vbBSInsideSolid**. This property does not work if the **BorderWidth** property which determines the width of the line is not 1. This is a limitation of the hardware. If you do wish to create a wide dashed line, you have to draw many lines of width 1 adjacent to each other.

You can move a line to a new position by selecting it and dragging. You can also alter the position of either end by selecting the line and then dragging one of its end points, which are indicated by squares at either end of the line.

The Shape Control

A **Shape** control can assume a variety of predefined shapes:

- Rectangle (with square or rounded corners).
- Square (with square or rounded corners).
- Oval.
- Circle.

The default shape is the rectangle, but other shapes can be selected by changing the value of the **Shape** property.

Properties of the Shape control

The **Shape** control shares many properties with other controls, such as **Name**, **Left**, **Top**, **Height**, and **Width**. In addition it has four properties for controlling its appearance.

Table 16.3 *Properties of the **Shape** control.*

Property	Description
BackColor	The colour of the enclosed area of the shape.
BackStyle	If set to 0 the shape is transparent. If set to 1, the default, the shape is opaque.
FillColor	The colour of hatching drawn over the background colour.
FillStyle	How the hatching is applied.

If the **BackStyle** property indicates that the shape is transparent, the **BackColor** property is irrelevant.

The **FillStyle** property determines how a shape is filled. If the **FillStyle** is set to transparent the **FillColor** property is ignored, except for the container form.

Table 16.4 *The **FillStyle** property.*

Constant	Value	Description
vbFSSolid	0	Solid fill.
vbFSTransparent	1	Transparent.
vbHorizontalLine	2	Horizontal lines.
vbVerticalLine	3	Vertical lines.
vbUpwardDiagonal	4	Diagonals up to the left.
vbDownwardDiagonal	5	Diagonals down to the left.
vbCross	6	Cross hatched with horizontal and vertical lines.
vbDiagonalCross	7	Cross hatched with diagonal lines.

The co-ordinate system

You can create many of the graphics you need at design time and put them in the right place by dragging and dropping. You can also add graphics at run-time using a set of methods covered later in this chapter, but before doing so it is essential to understand the co-ordinate system used by Visual Basic.

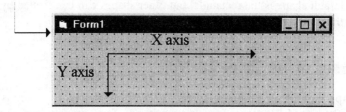

Fig 16.4 *The co-ordinate system.*

- The **Left** property refers to the co-ordinate of the left side of a control.
- The **Top** property refers to the co-ordinate of the top of the control.

The default unit used is the twip. 567 twips = 1 cm or 1440 inches. Twip stands for twentieth of a point. The top left of the screen is the 0,0 position.

The twip refers to the size when the image is printed. The size on the screen is dependent on the size and type of the monitor. The co-ordinate frame used is that of the container. If the image is on a form, it is the form's co-ordinate system that is used.

Twips and other units

Twips are not always a convenient unit to use. You can change the units by altering the **ScaleMode** property of the container. If you are drawing directly on the form, it is the container. The possible settings are shown in table 16.5.

Table 16.5 Changing units.

Constants	Value	Description
vbUser	0	User-defined.
vbTwips	1	Twips - the default. 1440 twips = 1 inch.
vbPoints	2	Points - 72 points = 1 inch.
vbPixels	3	Pixels.
vbCharacters	4	Characters. When printed a character is 1/16 inch high and 1/12 inch wide.
vbInches	5	Inches.
vbMillimeters	6	Millimetres.
vbCentimeters	7	Centimetres.

If you set **ScaleMode** to zero you need to set the limits of your working area using the **ScaleLeft, ScaleTop, ScaleWidth** and **ScaleHeight** properties. If you set any of these properties, **ScaleMode** is automatically set to **vbUser**.

Using graphics methods

You can create your own graphics at run-time using a set of methods as listed in table 16.6:

We are going to look at these methods in more detail, but one important fact to notice is that the arguments for the co-ordinates in all of the methods listed are single precision not integer.

Table 16.6 *Graphics methods.*

Method	Description
Cls	Clear all graphics.
Pset	Set the colour of an individual pixel.
Point	Return the colour of a pixel.
Line	Draw a line, rectangle or filled-in box.
Circle	Draw a circle, ellipse or arc.

Controlling individual pixels

[object.]Pset(x, y)[,colour]

For example:

Form1.Pset (70,50) , (127, 0, 255)

[object.]Point(x, y)

For example:

Point1 = Point(20.5,307.4)

If the colour argument is not used with **Pset,** the pixel is assigned the foreground colour (**ForeColor**). For all of these methods, if the object argument is not specified, the current object is used.

The Line method

The **Line** method draws a line between two specified points.

[object.]Line[(x1, y1)]-(x2, y2)[,colour]

If the object is not specified the current object is used.

Form1.Line(200,550)-(600,600)

Line -(800,700)

The first pair of co-ordinates is optional; if they are omitted, the current position is used in place of the missing co-ordinates.

The code shown below draws the lines shown in fig 16.5:

```
Private Sub Form_Click( )
For c = 1 To 10
    Form1.DrawWidth = c * 2
    Form1.ForeColor = RGB(Rnd * 255, Rnd * 255, Rnd * 255)
    Line (100, c * 200)-(100 + c * 500, c * 200)
```

> *Next c*
> *End Sub*

The width of the line drawn depends on the **DrawWidth** property. The colour can be set in two ways, either by specifying it as a parameter to the **Line** method or by setting the **ForeColor** property. The **RGB** function is a very useful function for specifying colour. It requires three parameters, the red, green and blue components of the colour. The **Rnd** function returns a random number between 0 and 1, if this is multiplied by 255, it produces a number between 0 and 255. The effect of this is to give each of the lines a different randomly chosen colour.

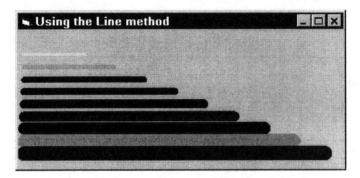

*Fig 16.5 Using the **Line** method.*

- The foreground colour is the colour of drawn objects, such as lines and squares.
- The background colour is the colour of the background on which objects are drawn.

The **Step** keyword indicates that the following co-ordinates are relative to the current position.

> *Line (200, 300) - (400,100) is equivalent to **Line**(200,300) - **Step**(200, -200)*

A rectangle of side 50 is drawn using the example below:

> *Line (100,100) - **Step**(50, 0)*
> *Line - **Step**(0,50)*
> *Line - **Step**(-50,0)*
> *Line - **Step**(0,-50)*

Drawing boxes

Stick and filled boxes are drawn using the **Line** statement by using the **B** parameter.

> *Line(100, 100) - **Step**(150, 150) , , **B***

This statement draws a rectangle. The first co-ordinates are the upper left corner and the second the bottom right.

The box can be filled using the **F** parameter after the **B**

> *Line(100, 100) - Step(150, 150) , , BF*

A stick box has an outline only. A filled box has a colour and hides whatever it sit on.

The Circle method

The **Circle** method can be used to draw circles, ellipses, arcs and pie shaped wedges. This method has many parameters, listed in table 16.7, fortunately you usually do not need to use them all. The general form of the **Circle** method is:

> *object.Circle Step (x, y), radius, colour, start, end, aspect*

Table 16.7 The parameters of the Circle method.

Parameter	Description
object	Optional. This specifies the container object which the graphic is to be drawn on. If it is omitted the form which has the focus is used as the object.
Step	Optional. If this parameter is used, the co-ordinates of the centre of the circle are relative to the current position.
(x, y)	Two **Single** precision values specifying the centre of the graphic.
radius	A **Single** precision value giving the radius of the graphic.
colour	Optional. A **Long** integer determining the colour of the graphics outline.
start, end	Optional. **Single** precision values which are required when drawing a pie shape of a part of a circle or ellipse. The positions give the start and end positions in radians.
aspect	Optional. When drawing an ellipse you need to specify this parameter which determines the aspect ratio of the ellipse.

The best way to learn how to use the **Circle** method is to look at a few examples.

Drawing circles and ellipses

To draw a circle only three parameters are needed, for example:

> *Circle(700,300), 200*

This line will draw a circle of radius 200 with its centre at co-ordinates 700, 300. If the **Step** keyword is used the centre of the circle is relative to the current co-ordinates given by the **CurrentX** and **CurrentY** properties.

The key difference between drawing circles and ellipses is the aspect parameter which is the ratio of the vertical to horizontal dimensions. The aspect ratio must be a positive floating point number.

> *Circle (300,400), 100, , , , 2*

This command draws an ellipse which has a horizontal width of 100. Since the aspect ratio is 2 the vertical height is 2x100 = 200. The centre is at 300, 400.

If you want to fill in the ellipse, the **FillStyle** property for the container object must be used. The program example below draws the ellipses shown in fig 16.6.

```
Private Sub Form_Click( )
    CurrentX = 200
    CurrentY = 600
    For c = 0 To 7
        FillStyle = c
        Circle Step(400, 0), 350, , , , 3
    Next c
End Sub
```

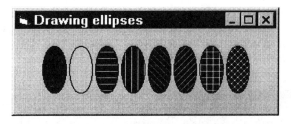

Fig 16.6 Drawing ellipses.

The ellipses are drawn on the currently active form. It gives your application more flexibility if you specify explicitly the container for the graphics. The code shown below does this and produces exactly the same output as fig 16.6.

```
Private Sub Form_Click( )
    Form1.CurrentX = 200
    Form1.CurrentY = 600
    For c = 0 To 7
        Form1.FillStyle = c
        Form1.Circle Step(400, 0), 350, , , , 3
    Next c
End Sub
```

Drawing arcs and pies

The versatile **Circle** method can also be used to draw arcs and pie shapes. The starting and end points for the arc or pie need to be specified. As shown in fig 16.7, the eastern direction is taken as the zero position. Arcs and pies are always drawn anti-clockwise and start and end positions specified in radians. 2π radians are equal to 360 degrees.

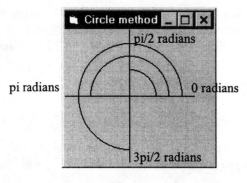

*Fig 16.7 The **Circle** method.*

The code shown below draws the arc and pi shapes shown in fig 16.8.

```
Private Sub Form_Click( )
    Const pi = 3.142
    Form1.Circle (1000, 500), 400, , pi / 2, 3 * pi / 2
    Form1.Circle (2000, 500), 400, , -pi / 2, -3 * pi /2
End Sub
```

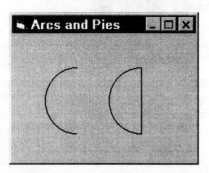

Fig 16.8 Drawing arcs and pies.

The only differences between the two **Circle** methods used are the x, y co-ordinates so that they are not drawn on top of each other and the minus sign before the start and end parameters.

The Image and PictureBox controls

The sort of graphics that you can create at run-time are quite limited. It is more likely that you will want to incorporate existing graphics into your applications. To do this you need to use a container control. The most commonly used controls for this are the **Image** and **PictureBox** controls.

Image controls and **PictureBox** controls are very similar, but there are several important differences:

- **Image** controls do not have the **AutoSize** property, but they automatically resize to fit the image.
- **Image** controls have the **Stretch** property, which will resize the control to fit the image.
- If you simply want to display a picture, the **Image** control is the best choice, since the **Image** control uses less system resources than a **PictureBox**.
- **Image** controls can only contain pictures. They cannot contain other controls or run-time graphics.

Supported image formats

The graphics that you incorporate into your application must be one of the following types:

Table 16.8 Supported graphics formats.

Format	File extension
Bitmap.	BMP.
Icon.	ICO.
Metafile.	WMF.
Enhanced metafile.	EMF.
JPEG.	JPG.
GIF.	GIF.

Icon files are a special type of bitmap with a maximum size of 32 by 32 pixels. Metafiles are usually smaller than comparable bitmaps since images are stored as a sequence of lines and basic shapes rather than on a bit by bit basis as is the case in BMP files. The file types supported include the most common types, if the type you want is not available it is straightforward to convert between file types using many popular drawing applications such as CorelDraw.

The file containing the graphic is specified in the Properties window by the **Picture** property. By selecting this property and double clicking, you can browse through the directories on your disks and select the file containing the graphic.

The Stretch property

This is a property of **Image** controls only. The default value for the **Stretch** property is **False**. When an image is imported the **Image** control resizes itself to fit the image. If the **Image** control is resized, the image remains the same size. However, if **Stretch** is **True**, the image resizes itself so that it fits the size of the **Image** control. The screen below shows the same images in three differently sized **Image** controls.

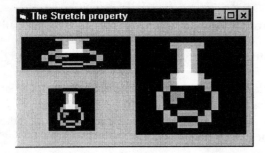

Fig 16.9 The Stretch property.

The AutoSize property

An especially useful property of **PictureBox** control is the **AutoSize** property. When **AutoSize = True** the control automatically resizes to fit the picture. When **AutoSize = False** the picture is not re-scaled to fit the size of the **PictureBox** - if the **PictureBox** is shrunk, the portion of the image displayed is reduced.

Fig 16.10 The AutoSize property.

Fig 16.10 shows the same image fully displayed in the right **PictureBox**, since the **AutoSize** property is **True**. In the left **PictureBox** only a portion of the image is shown since **AutoSize = False**.

Adding a picture at run-time

At run-time pictures can be added by:

- The **LoadPicture** function.
- Copying a picture from one object to another.

The **LoadPicture** function has the following form:

> *Shape1.**Picture** = **LoadPicture**("C:\Photos\Holiday\Paris1.bmp")*

This replaces the existing image.
Pictures can be erased by:

> *Shape1.Picture = **LoadPicture**("")*

Pictures can be copied using normal assignment statements:

> *Shape1.**Picture** = Shape2.**Picture***

This also replaces the existing picture.
The next example uses a **CommonDialog** control to browse for an image file and to display it in an **Image** control. The **CommonDialog** control can be placed anywhere on the form since it is not visible at run-time. The working application is shown in fig 16.11:

Fig 16.11 Loading pictures at run-time.

The only code required is in the button click event:

```
Private Sub Command1_Click( )
    CommonDialog1.Filter = "Pictures | *.bmp; *.ico; *.jpg; *.wmf; *.emf"
    CommonDialog1.ShowOpen
    Image1.Picture = LoadPicture(CommonDialog1.filename)
End Sub
```

The **CommonDialog Filter** property determines which types of files are displayed in the Open File dialog box. The text which is displayed in the *Files of type* **TextBox** is *Pictures*, the extensions of the displayed file types are listed next, in this case all of the supported graphics formats. The **LoadPicture** method is used to load and display the image.

17

Mouse and Keyboard Events

Introduction

When a mouse is moved or one of its buttons clicked an event happens, similarly when a button on the keyboard is pressed an event occurs. The processing of these events is a crucial area in Visual Basic. Since the behaviour of the keyboard and the mouse is closely related to Windows 95, mouse and keyboard events are unchanged from the previous version of Visual Basic.

In this chapter you will learn about:

- The keyboard events.
- The mouse events.
- The mouse button events.
- Dragging and dropping objects.
- The effect of the **Shift**, **Ctrl** and **Alt** buttons on using the mouse.

Keyboard events

The main keyboard events are:

- **KeyPress.**
- **KeyDown.**
- **KeyUp.**

When a printable ASCII character is pressed, the event sequence is **KeyDown**, **KeyPress**, **KeyUp**. However, when an non printable key, such as one of the arrowed keys is pressed, the sequence is **KeyDown**, **KeyUp**. The **KeyPress** event does not occur. This can be demonstrated by the following example, where the event name is added to a list box whenever that event occurs.:

> ***Private Sub** List1_**KeyDown**(KeyCode **As Integer**, Shift **As Integer**)*
>   *List1.**AddItem** "KeyDown"*
> ***End Sub***
>
> ***Private Sub** List1_**KeyUp**(KeyCode **As Integer**, Shift **As Integer**)*
>   *List1.**AddItem** "KeyUp"*
> ***End Sub***
>
> ***Private Sub** List1_**KeyPress**(KeyAscii **As Integer**)*
>   *List1.**AddItem** "KeyPress"*
> ***End Sub***

The running application is shown in fig 17.1:

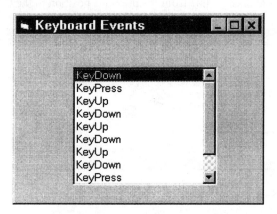

Fig 17.1 The keyboard events

Note that the parameters supplied to the **KeyUp** and **KeyDown** events are different and indicate the status of the **Shift** key.

Mouse events

There are three mouse events that Visual Basic recognises as shown in table 17.1:

Table 17.1 Mouse events.

Mouse Event	Description
MouseDown	A mouse button is pressed.
MouseUp	A pressed mouse button is released.
MouseMove	The mouse is moved from its current position.

The same **MouseUp** and **MouseDown** events occur irrespective of which mouse button is used. In order to find out which button is used, you must refer to an argument passed by Visual Basic to the event handler.

The MouseMove event

Whenever the mouse moves a **MouseMove** event occurs. The number of events which can be detected depends on the speed of your computer. Only one line of code is needed to produce the application shown running in fig 17.2:

> ***Private Sub** Form_MouseMove(Button As Integer, Shift As Integer,*
> ***X** As Single, Y As Single)*
>
> > ***Line** -(X, Y)*
> > ***End Sub***

The **Line** method draws a line from the previous position to the current one.

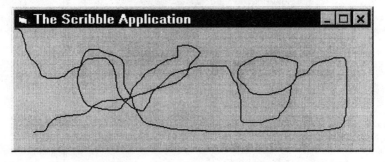

Fig 17.2 The Scribble application.

Mouse event arguments

The mouse events all use the same arguments:

Table 17.2 Mouse event arguments.

Argument	Description
Button	A bit field in which the 3 least significant bits give the status of the buttons.
Shift	A bit field in which the least significant buttons give the status of the **Shift, Ctrl** and **Alt** buttons.
X, Y	Location of the mouse pointer.

The program shown below can be used to draw lines on the form. The button which has been pressed is indicated by the first parameter. Visual Basic automatically produces the outline procedure, including the list of parameters that are passed to it.

> *Private Sub Form_MouseDown (Button As Integer, Shift As Integer,*
> *X As Single, Y As Single)*
>
> *Line - (X, Y)*
> *End Sub*

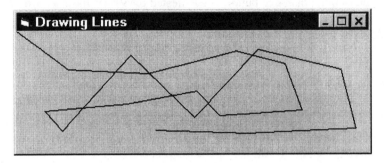

Fig 17.3 Drawing lines

The **Line** method is used to draw a line from the present point to the specified point. Every time the **MouseDown** event occurs, a line is drawn to the new position as shown. In this example, it does not matter which mouse button is pressed.

The click events

The following events are associated with the mouse buttons:

- The **Click** and **DblClick** events occur as a result of using the mouse buttons.
- The **Click** and **DblClick** events do not differentiate which mouse button has been pressed.
- The same event handler is used irrespective of which button is used.

Windows measures the time between successive clicks and therefore is able to differentiate between single and double clicks. This time period is configurable using the Windows Control Panel.

The MouseDown, MouseUp events

When a mouse button is pressed, a **MouseDown** event occurs. When it is released a **MouseUp** event occurs. The usage of these events differs from the **Click** and **DblClick** events in that they allow the programmer to determine which button has been pressed.

> *Private Sub Command1_MouseDown (Button As Integer, Shift As Integer,*
> *X As Single, Y As Single)*

These events receive as parameters a value indicating which button has been pressed and the status of the **Shift, Alt** and **Ctrl** keys.

The Button argument

The *Button* parameter indicates the status of each of the 3 mouse buttons. This can be one of three values **vbLeftButton, vbRightButton,** or **vbMiddleButton.**

If you press more than one button this is treated by Visual Basic as two events. If you want to differentiate between the buttons, which all generate the same event, you need to do so by testing the value in the event handler.

The Shift, Ctrl and Alt arguments

The **Shift** argument is used in a similar way to the *Button* argument:

- **Shift = vbShiftMask** The **Shift** button is pressed.
- **Shift = vbCtrlMask.** The **Ctrl** button is pressed.
- **Shift = vbAltmask.** The **Alt** button is pressed.

Dragging and dropping

Dragging and dropping are the techniques used to move a control from one position to another using the mouse.

A control is dragged by moving the pointer onto the control and pressing the left mouse button. As the mouse is dragged the control moves. When the button is released the control is dropped into its new position.

Visual Basic fully supports drag and drop using one method, **Drag** , and two events, **DragOver** and **DragDrop.**

The Drag method

If you want to drag a picture you should use the **Drag** method in the source code for the **MouseDown** event. The general form of the **Drag** method is:

*CtrlName.**Drag** action*

The optional *action* parameter specifies the type of drag action taken.

*Table 17.3 The **Action** parameter of the **Drag** method.*

Value	Action
vbCancel	Cancel dragging.
vbBeginDrag	Start dragging the control.
vbEndDrag	Drop the control.

The default value for the action parameter is **vbBeginDrag** (start dragging the control).

The **MouseDown** event for the control which is to be dragged and dropped must contain a statement which allows the control to be dragged. When the mouse button is released the control is dropped into its new location.

```
Private Sub Picture1_MouseDown (Button As Integer, Shift As Integer,
                                          X As Single, Y As Single)
' Starts dragging the control
    Picture1.Drag vbBeginDrag
End Sub

Private Sub Picture1_MouseUp (Button As Integer, Shift As Integer,
                                        X As Single, Y As Single)
' Drops the control
    Picture1.Drag vbEndDrag
End Sub
```

The form must be prepared to respond to the dropping of the control by using the **DragDrop** event. If you do not do this you will be able to drag the control, but when you release the button to drop the dragged control, it returns to its original position.

```
Private Sub Form_DragDrop (source As Control, X As Single, Y As Single)
    Source.Move X, Y
End Sub
```

The **DragDrop** event positions the control with its top left corner at the specified co-ordinates.

The DragIcon property

When a control is dragged, a grey rectangle is used to represent it. The drag icon which is displayed can be changed by using the **DragIcon** property. Particularly useful, if a picture is being dragged is to change the **DragIcon** property to the same icon as the picture that is being dragged. This has the effect of showing the picture itself moving as it is dragged.

```
Private Sub Form_Load ( )
    Picture1.DragIcon = Picture1.Picture
End Sub
```

The DragOver event

The **DragIcon** property can be used in conjunction with the **DragOver** event to indicate that the control being dragged is in an area of the form that does not accept a drop. The usual way of doing this is to change the **DragIcon** property into an appropriate symbol such as a stop sign when it passes over the forbidden area - and back to normal when it leaves.

There is no code to prevent you from trying to drop the picture into this invalid area, but if you do so, nothing happens as there is no code in *Picture2*'s **DrapDrop** event processing.

```
Private Sub Picture2_DragOver (Source As Control), X As Single, Y As
                                            Single, State As Integer)
    If State = 0 Then
        Picture1.DragIcon = LoadPicture(c:\vb\icons\stopicon.ico)
    If State = 1 Then
        Picture1.DragIcon = Picture1.Picture
End Sub
```

18
Databases

Introduction

Most serious Windows applications use a database. Visual Basic version 4 allowed you to write applications which not only used databases but also allowed you to create your own databases without the need to have a separate database application such as Access. Version 5 has increased the number of databases which are supported and the user interface for creating and managing databases has been greatly improved. The Visual Data Manager has been included which covers all aspects of database management. A Data Form Wizard has also been introduced which simplifies the building of user interfaces for database applications.

Visual Basic offers an extensive range of data-aware controls which can be used to design your own specialised data forms if the Data Form Wizard does not offer exactly what you need.

One of the main differences between the CCE and commercial version of Visual Basic is the CCE does not include the **Data** control which is essential for database development.

In this chapter you will learn about:

- Relational databases.
- Using the Visual Data Manager.
- Using the Data Form Wizard.
- Using the data-aware controls.

Database design and implementation is a huge area and the Visual Basic manuals cover over 1000 pages on this topic, in addition to suggesting further reading! If you are not designing database applications full-time this can seem very daunting. This chapter covers all of the essential features that you need to know to develop many serious database applications fast.

What are databases?

Virtually all organisations need to keep a track of information. They need to know who their customers are, what their current stock levels are, employee records need to be maintained. It is hard to think of any organisation which does not have an extensive need to keep track of data concerning its employees, customers and business. It is essential that this data is organised so that it can be recovered easily. A manual filing system will be organised with separate filing cabinets containing information specific areas, and the filing cabinets being divided into separate folders. Databases act as electronic filing cabinets imposing a structure and organisation on data so that you can easily find the information you want. Databases also allow you to enter new data in the right place so that it can be easily found.

There are a variety of database models. In recent years, multi-dimensional databases have grown in importance, but by far the most widely used type of database are relational. Visual Basic only supports the relational database model. Fortunately all of the widely used databases such as Access and Dbase are relational.

Relational databases

In a relational database all information is stored in tables such as one shown in table 18.1:

Table 18.1 Tables in relational databases.

First Name	Second name	Address
Bill	Smedley	17 Church Way, Northampton
Sally	Smedley	17 Church Way, Northampton
Tom	Schwartz	15 Waltham Close, Weston Favell

- Each of the squares in the table is a field.
- Each row is called a record.

If you want to add another person to the table you just add another row.

Key Fields

If you want your database to give you information on a particular person, your application will need to search through the table until it finds what you want. You can speed this up by specifying in your database design that you want to use the second name field as a key field. The database will construct an index table which will greatly reduce the time taken to find the records you want.

You can request as many key fields as you want, but although they are invisible to you they will take up space on your disk. It is easily possible for the indexes to be larger than the tables they are indexing, so they should be added with care. Although adding key fields to your application will speed up the access time when searching through the database it will take longer to update the database if you add a record, since your application will need to update the indexes.

When you are choosing a key field you should choose a field which is unique if possible, that is there are never two records which have the same value in this field. This is the reason that companies like to assign unique numbers to their customers. It makes sure that the right person can be easily identified and simplifies the design of their databases.

Normalisation

In the table shown in table 18.1, there are two records which have the same address field. This will occur frequently if you are keeping a record of names and addresses. It is good database design to put the addresses into a separate table since the address is long, and space can be saved by storing it once. It is also easy to have two slightly different versions of the same address which are both correct, perhaps one includes the region as well as the city. This can be confusing as well as annoying. I currently receive three copies of a popular free computing magazine each of which has slight variants of my address.

A better way to store the information in table 18.1 is shown in table 18.2.

Table 18.2 *Handling a one-to-many relationship.*

First name	Second name	Address code
Bill	Smedley	123
Sally	Smedley	123
Tom	Schwartz	456

Address code	Address
123	17 Church Way...
456	15 Waltham Close...

The connection between the two tables is the address code which is common to the tables. There is a one-to-many relationship between the address and the people, since for each address there may be many people.

The process of splitting the information into multiple tables to avoid duplication is called normalisation.

Many-to-many relationships

Sometimes in a database there will be a many-to-many relationship within the data, for example, if you are maintaining a list of names and addresses it is likely that there will be more than one person living at an address but it is also possible that one person will have more than one address. This is a common relationship in databases and can be handled as shown in table 18.3.

Table 18.3 Handling a many-to-many relationship.

First name	Second name	Person code
Bill	Smedley	1
Sally	Smedley	2
Tom	Schwartz	3

Address code	Person code
123	1
123	2
456	3
789	3

Address code	Address
123	17 Church Way.
456	15 Waltham Close.
789	The Old Bakehouse.

In this example, *Bill Smedley* and *Sally Smedley* both live at *17 Church Way*, which has an address code of *123*. The address code *123* is listed against the two person codes of *1* and *2*. *Tom Schwartz* owns both *15 Waltham Close* and *The Old Bakehouse*. His person code of *3*, is listed against the address codes *456* and *789*.

Relational databases provide ways of performing enquiries on data stored in this form so that you can easily find out who lives at a particular address, or who owns a particular property. You can also easily list all the owners of all the properties.

What databases does Visual Basic support?

The Microsoft Jet database engine which is used in Access is built into Visual Basic and Visual Basic therefore supports all of the database types that Access does. Supported databases are:

Table 18.4 Supported databases

Database	Version
Access	2.0 and 7.0.
Dbase	5.0, IV, III.
FoxPro	3.0, 2.6, 2.5, 2.0.
Paradox	5.0, 4.x, 3.x.
ODBC	generic ODBC databases.
Excel, Lotus 1-2-3, text.	-

ODBC is short for Open Database Connectivity. ODBC databases include remote database environments including Microsoft SQL server and Oracle. In addition you can access Excel, Lotus 1-2-3 and standard ASCII text files as if they were databases.

Creating a database

In this section we are going to create a database and use the Data Form Wizard. The first database we are going to build contains some details of animals in a zoo. It has only one table which has four fields:

- The name of the animal.
- The age of the animal.
- The type of animal.
- The name of the keeper.

To create a database:

- Select the **File | New Project** menu item.
- Choose the **Standard EXE** project option.
- Select the **Add-Ins | Visual Data Manager** menu option. This will display the **VisData** menu.
- Select the **File | New** option.
- Select **Microsoft Access**.
- Select **Version 7.0**. This is the latest version of Access.

The form displayed is shown in fig 18.1

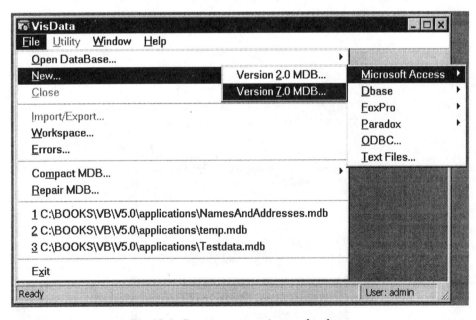

Fig 18.1 *Creating a new Access database.*

Call the newly created database *Zoo* as shown in fig 18.2.

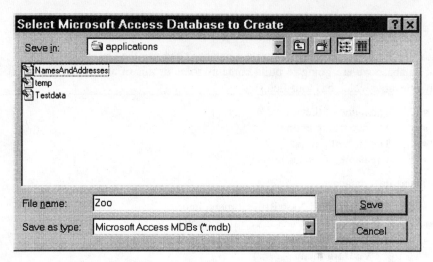

Fig 18.2 Creating a new Access database.

The database shell now exists but no tables or fields have yet been created and no data has been entered.

Adding tables to the database

To add the single table to the *Zoo* database:

- Display the Database window by selecting the **Window | Database Window** menu option.
- Right click the mouse over the **Properties** entry on the Database window.
- Select the **New Table** option as shown in fig 18.3.

Fig 18.3 Creating a new table.

The fields the table contains must be defined before data can be added:

- Specify the table name as *Animals* as shown in fig 18.4.
- Click on the **Add Field** button to insert the first field in the table.

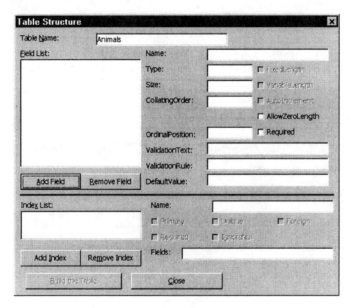

Fig 18.4 *Adding fields to the table.*

The Add Field form is shown below in fig 18.5:

- Give the first field a name of *Name*.
- Set the type to **Text**.
- Set the size to 20 characters.

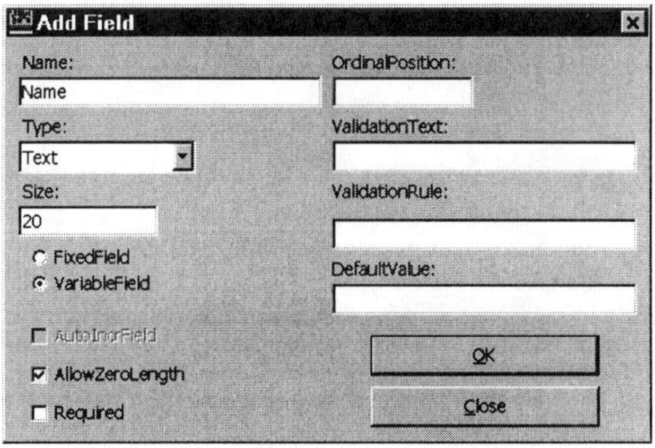

Fig 18.5 *Adding new fields to a table.*

Click on the **OK** button. The **Name** field is cleared ready for you to enter the next fields. These fields have the following properties shown in table 18.5:

Table 18.5 *Field names and properties.*

Name	Type	Size
Age	Integer	2
AnimalType	Text	20
KeeperName	Text	25

When you have entered all this data click the **Close** button.
The Table Structure form should be similar to the one shown in fig 18.6.

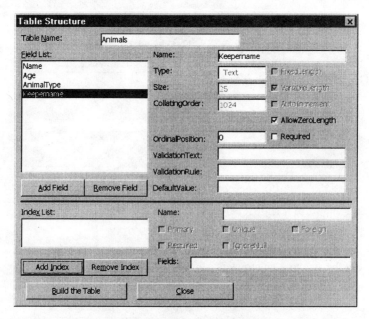

Fig 18.6 *The completed table.*

Adding an Index

To add an index to this table click on the **Add Index** button. The form shown in fig 18.7 is displayed. To make the **Name** field an index, double click on the **Name** field in the **Available Fields** list. Give the index the name *NameIndex* as shown.

- As a default, the key is the primary key and each entry in this field must be unique. Click on the **Close** button to return to the Table Structure Window.

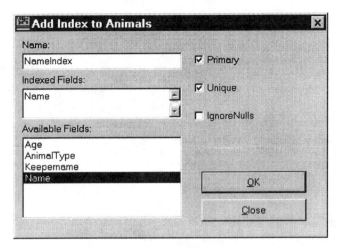

Fig 18.7 Adding an index to a table.

- Click on the **Build the Table** button to finish the design phase of the table and to enter it into the database.

The Database window will now be displayed.

Adding data to the table

The database has been created, a single table has been added to it, and the fields in that table have been defined. The next stage is to add data to the table:

- Select the table *Animals* in the Database window and right click the mouse to display the speed menu.
- Select the **Open** option to add data to the database. The form shown in fig 18.8 is displayed.

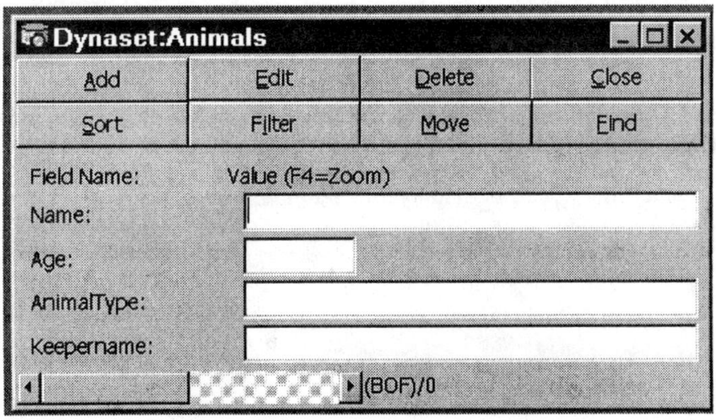

Fig 18.8 Adding data to a table.

- To add a new record to this table click on the **Add** button.

The form shown in fig 18.9 is displayed.

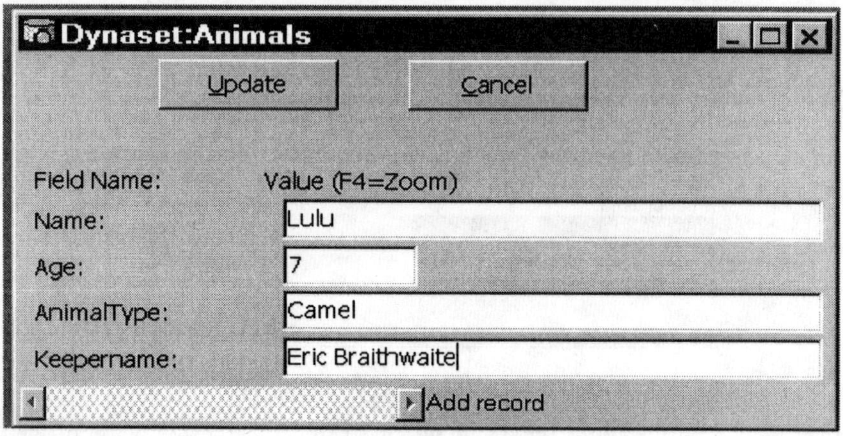

Fig 18.9 Adding data to the Animals table.

To insert the data into the database click on the **Update** button. Repeat this process for every record you want to enter into the table.

As you enter records on the system note that you can page through the records on the system using the scroll bar at the bottom of the form. Add several records so that you can confirm that the application the Data Form Wizard creates functions correctly.

The database has now been designed, created and data entered into it. To view and modify this data, an application has to be written.

The Data Form Wizard

To write an application close the Visual Data Manager. If you have not used the Data Form Wizard before you need to make it available to your design desktop.

- Select the **Add-Ins | Add-Ins Manager** menu option.
- Click on the **VB Data Form Wizard** check box.
- The Data Form Wizard will now be available from the **Add-Ins** menu. Select this option.

An initial welcome screen is displayed. You can prevent this from being shown in future by clicking on a check box on the bottom left of the form. The form shown in fig 18.10 is then displayed.

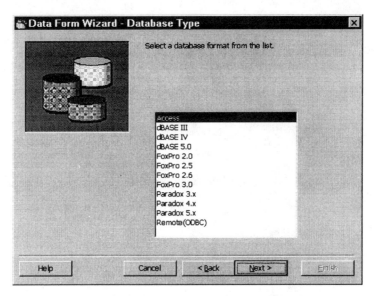

Fig 18.10 *Selecting the database type.*

The database we have just created is an Access database, so you should select this option.

Click on the **Next** button to display the menu shown in fig 18.11.

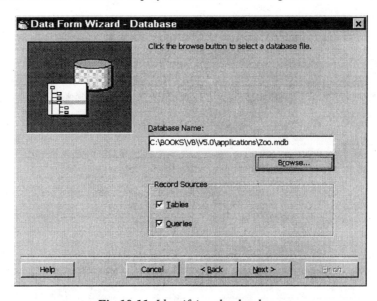

Fig 18.11 *Identifying the database.*

Only Access databases are available since we have specified that the database is of this type. Select the *Zoo* database. If necessary click on the **Browse** button to locate the database.

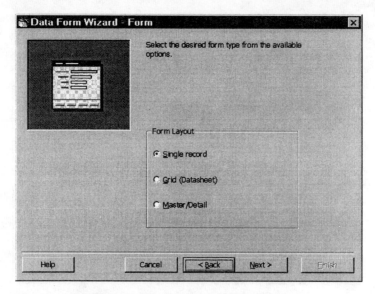

Fig 18.12 Choosing the display format.

The Data Form Wizard allows you to select a variety of formats for displaying the information you have requested. In this case we are going to select the simplest **Single record** option, which will display only one record at a time. Click on the **Next** button to move to the next stage in the form design.

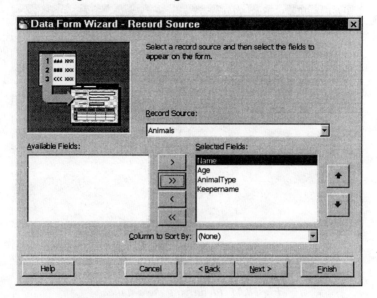

Fig 18.13 Selecting fields to be displayed.

This form allows you to specify which fields in the record you wish to display. Click on the down arrow on the right of the **Record Source ComboBox** to see all the available tables. In this case there is only one table called *Animals*, which you should select. A list of all the available fields is displayed in the **Available Fields ListBox**. (To select the fields individually click on the right pointing arrows. To select all fields click on the double right pointing arrows. To deselect click on the left facing arrows.) Select all of the fields.

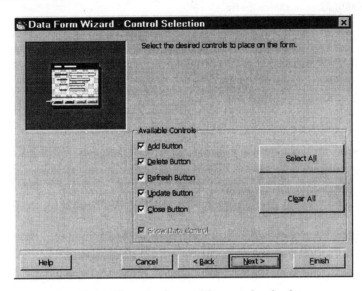

Fig 18.14 Choosing control buttons for the form.

The Data Form Wizard can include controls on the form it creates which allow you to navigate through the database. In this case select all of the buttons.

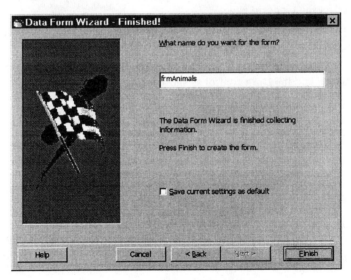

Fig 18.15 The wizard has finished.

The final stage of the form design is now complete and ready to run.

Running the application

The completed form is shown in fig 18.16.

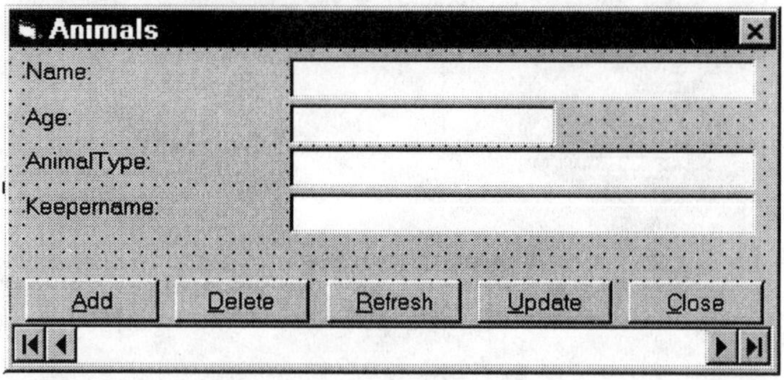

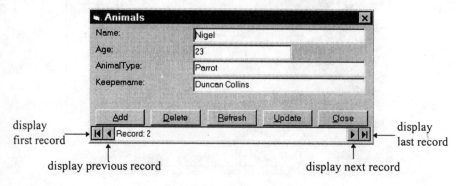

Fig 18.16 The completed form.

There are a few more stages before the application is ready to run. The default form is still *Form1*:

- To delete *Form1* from your application, display the project window and select it.
- Choose the **Project | Remove Form1.frm** menu option.
- To make the form created by the Data Form Wizard the default form which is displayed on startup select the **Project | Project1 Properties** option.
- Select the **General** page.
- Set the **Startup Object** to *frmAnimals* (or whatever you have called the form).

The application is now ready to run and you can navigate through the database using the buttons and the **Data** control as shown in fig 18.17.

Fig 18.17 The running application.

Implementing a many-to-many relationship

Databases with one table are very straightforward to develop using the VisData and the Data Form Wizard. You can develop multi form applications using these tools, but you need to know SQL (normally pronounced *sequel*). Structured Query Language is a standard language used to manipulate relational databases. If you are serious about developing relational database applications you need to know SQL. This book is not a tutorial in SQL but it does show how it can be used to create queries using Visual Basic.

The application we are going to develop is a variant of the zoo application which has the table structure shown in table 18.6.

Table 18.6 *The database tables.*

Animal Table

Animal code	Name	Type	Age	Food
A1	Lulu	Zebra	7	Grass
A2	Bill	Lion	15	Meat
A3	Samantha	Zebra	8	Grass
A4	Percy	Parrot	56	Seeds

Keeper Table

Keeper code	Name	Grade
K1	Tom Simmons	Senior
K2	Fiaz Hussein	Senior
K3	Sally Patel	Junior

Index Table

Keeper code	Animal code
K1	A1
K1	A2
K3	A2
K2	A3

In this database a keeper may look after more than one animal, but an individual animal may also be looked after by more than one keeper.

Creating the database

To create this database:

- Start a new **Standard EXE** project.
- Select the **Add-Ins | Visual Data Manager** menu option.
- Select the **File | New** option.
- Select **Microsoft Access Version 7.0**.
- When prompted for the name of the database, type *AnimalsAndKeepers*.

The database has now been created, the three tables must be added to it in turn:

- Right click over the **Properties** entry in the Database window.
- Select the new table option from the speed menu.
- Give the table the name *Animals*.

- Click on the **Add Field** button to add the fields, choosing an appropriate size.

Repeat this process to add the two other tables *Keeper* and *Index* to the database. To add the data to the tables:

- Choose each table in turn from the Database window.
- Right click the mouse
- Choose the **Open** option from the speed menu to add the data to the table.

The database has been created and the data added. Since there are several tables in this database you will need to write some SQL to perform enquiries on the table. If the SQL window is not displayed you should select the **Window | SQL Statement** menu option. The SQL Window is shown in fig 18.18.

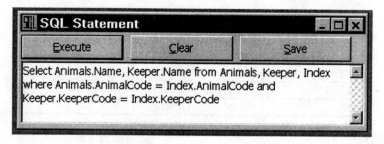

Fig 18.18 *The SQL window.*

The SQL statement below displays the name of every animal and its keeper:

> ***Select*** *Animals.Name, Keeper.Name* ***from*** *Animals, Keeper, Index*
> ***where*** *Animals.AnimalCode = Index.AnimalCode* ***and***
> *Keeper.KeeperCode = Index.KeeperCode*

To save this SQL statement click on **Save** and specify its name.

To create an application which will use this database and query it using the SQL statement:

- Exit VisData.
- Select the **Add-Ins | File Forms Wizard** option.
- Select the *AnimalsAndKeepers* database.
- When prompted for the **Record source** specify the name of the SQL statement you have created.
- Complete the application as before. Remember to make the form created by the Data Form Wizard the startup form.

The running application is shown in fig 18.19.

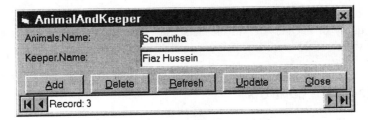

Fig 18.19 The running application.

The Data control

If you use the Data Form Wizard to create a form you can still modify it, but sometimes it is easier to create your own forms using the controls which Visual Basic provides.

The **Data** control connects your Visual Basic application to the database and opens a specified database table or a set of records based on an SQL query on the database:

- After the **Data** control has been connected to the database you can bind data-aware controls to the **Data** control.
- The data-aware controls connect fields of data in the database to the control.

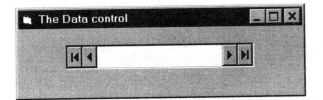

*Fig 18.20 The **Data** control.*

- If you click on the leftmost arrow, the first set of data which matches the enquiry made is displayed.
- The next arrow shows the previous data set. If the first set is displayed no action is taken.
- Similarly, the two right arrows move to the next set and the last set.

Properties of the Data control

There are two key properties of the **Data** control which allow you to connect the database and a table to the control.

- The **DataBaseName** property specify which database the control is connecting to.

- The **RecordSource** property can be either the name of a table or an SQL query or a QueryDef in the database. The **RecordSource** determines the source of the records which are available.

The data-aware controls

Visual Basic allows you to bind a few controls to particular fields in the record set. The controls you can use are:

- **TextBox**.
- **Image**.
- **PictureBox**.
- **CheckBox**.
- **Label**.

In addition there are three special controls which are data-aware variants of other controls available as custom controls. These controls are:

- **DBGrid**.
- **DBCombo**.
- **DBList**.

Properties for data-aware controls

There are three key properties for the data-aware controls which specify which field the control is to display:

- The **DataSource** property is the name of the data control.
- The **DataField** property is the name of the field that you are binding to.
- The **DataChanged** property indicates if the data has changed. This control is only available at run-time.

The best way to learn how to use these controls is to develop an application using them.

The Animals database

In this section we are going to construct a form which will allow us to browse through the *Animals* database.

The first stage is to create the form, which should look like the one shown in fig 18.21.

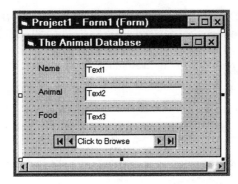

Fig 18.21 The completed design form.

The form consists of three **Label** controls, three **TextBox** controls and a **Data** control. To establish the links between the database and the application:

- Set the **DataBaseName** property of the **Data** control to *AnimalsAndKeepers*. You can browse through your folders to find this.
- Set the **RecordSource** property to *Animals*.
- Set the **DataSource** property of each of the **TextBox** controls to the name of the **Data** control, *Data1*.
- Set the **DataField** property of the three **TextBox** controls to the fields *Name*, *Animal* and *Food*. These are the fields which will be displayed.

The application is now ready to run. The running version is shown in fig 18.22.

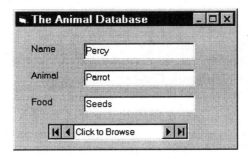

Fig 18.22 The running application.

Database methods

The only way which we have looked at of displaying information is by using the **Data** control or allowing the Data Form Wizard to create appropriate controls for us. However Visual Basic offers an extensive set of methods which allow you to have full control over your database application. All database applications must have at least one **Data** control, but if you want to create your own controls for viewing and manipulation data you can set the **Data** control's **Visible** property to **False**. It will still provide the connection between your application and a database, but will not allow the user to move through the record set.

The methods that you need to duplicate the functionality of the **Data** control are:

- **MoveNext.**
- **MoveFirst.**
- **MoveLast.**
- **MovePrevious.**

The previous application can be changed easily to use these methods as shown in fig 18.23:

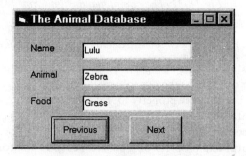

Fig 18.23 Using the MovePrevious and MoveNext methods.

The only code needed is in the click event for the two buttons:

```
Private Sub Command1_Click( )
    Data1.Recordset.MovePrevious
End Sub

Private Sub Command2_Click( )
    Data1.Recordset.MoveNext
End Sub
```

Remember that the **Data** control has not been deleted, just made invisible.

The BOF and EOF properties

One fault with the previous example is that if you are already displaying the first record and you click on previous an error occurs. A similar error occurs if you try and read past the end of the record set. Fortunately there are two properties which you can use to prevent the error from occurring:

- **BOF** (Beginning Of File) returns a value which is **True** if the current record position is before the record and **False** if the current position is on the first or subsequent records.

- **EOF** (End Of File) is **True** if the current position is after the end of the record set, otherwise it is **False**.

The lines of code in the *Previous* and *Next* button click events can be modified to use these properties and to prevent the errors occurring:

Private Sub Command1_Click( )
    If Not Data1.Recordset.BOF Then Data1.Recordset.MovePrevious
End Sub

Private Sub Command2_Click( )
    If Not Data1.Recordset.EOF Then Data1.Recordset.MoveNext
End Sub

Deleting and adding records

The current record can be deleted by using the **Delete** method, for example:

Data1.Recordset.Delete

If only the above line is used, the current record is deleted from the database, but remains displayed on the screen. Therefore it is a good idea to shift the focus to the next record by using the **MoveNext** method to display the next record or the first record if the end of the record set has been reached:

Data1.Recordset.MoveNext
If Data1.Recordset.EOF Then Data1.Recordset.MoveFirst

The **AddNew** method clears all the fields in a record in preparation for a new record to be added. After using **AddNew** the **Update** method is automatically invoked to save the data to the database, for example:

Data1.Recordset.AddNew

19
Menu and Toolbar Reference

Introduction

The menu system provides a comprehensive set of tools for developing applications. The four toolbars provide a shortcut way of accessing the most commonly used functions. There is nothing available via the toolbars that cannot be done using the menu.

In this chapter you will learn about:

- The menu.
- The function of the standard toolbar.

This chapter is intended as a reference to the essential features of the menu system and the toolbars. In the examples in earlier chapters there are many examples of using both the menu and toolbars. In addition to this chapter Visual Basic has excellent context sensitive help if you press **F1**.

The Print dialog box

The **Print** option in this menu offers several choices in the Print dialog box.
The **Range** options control the scope of the items that you print:

- **Selection.** Prints the currently selected code.
- **Current Module.** Prints the forms and code for the selected module.
- **Current Project**. Prints the forms and code for the whole project.

The **Print What** options determine what you can print:

- **Form Image** - prints an image of the form.

- **Code** - prints code.
- **Forms As Text** - prints the textual representation of the form.

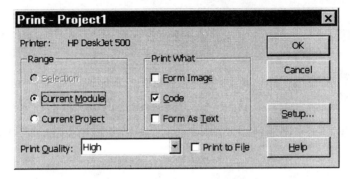

Fig 19.1 The Print dialog box.

The **Print Setup** option is standard in virtually all Windows applications and allows you to change how your printer behaves.

The Edit menu

The **Edit** menu has been considerably extended in this version of Visual Basic to include many additional useful functions. The first two options are shown in fig 19.2.

Fig. 19.2 Undoing actions.

When editing code it is easy to make mistakes, for example, to delete some important text. If you want to undo your previous action, click on the **Undo** option. The word following **Undo** (in this case **Insert Text**) indicates what the previous action was. You can undo many previous actions - I have never reached the limit on the number of actions you can undo. You can also choose to redo an action if you wish, after having undone it.

If you select text or controls on a form you can cut them, that is remove them to a temporary buffer with the **Cut** command, shown in fig 19.3. You can make a copy of the selected items without deleting it using the **Copy** option. If you wish to insert the selected material elsewhere select the **Paste** option.

Delete removes the selected item.

Select All allows you to select every control on a form or all the text in a file.

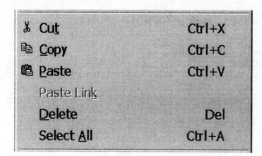

Fig. 19.3 *Cutting and pasting.*

One of the most commonly used functions of an editor is that it helps you to find the text you want, as shown in fig 19.4.

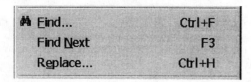

Fig. 19.4 *Finding text.*

Forgetting where you put some code is a particular problem with Visual Basic since your application may be made up of many different files. Fortunately the **Find** option allows you to specify the extent of your search as shown in fig 19.5.

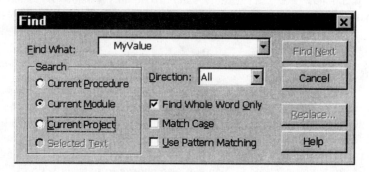

Fig. 19.5 *Specifying the scope of a find.*

You can either search only in one procedure, the current module, that is the current file, or all code files in the entire project.

Fig. 19.6 *Indenting text.*

It is standard procedure in programming to step a block of code one tab to the right if for example, it forms the body of a loop. This marks the code as being a block to the programmer. It makes no difference to how the application runs. The **Indent** option, shown in fig 19.6, moves either the current line of text or the selected text one tab position to the right. The **Outdent** option moves it to the left.

Fig. 19.7 Inserting text files.

Fig 19.7 shows the **Insert File** option, which allows you to write the contents of a text file to the current cursor position in you file.

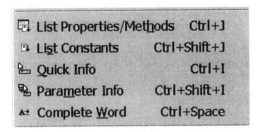

Fig. 19.8 Getting help.

The next set of five commands, shown in fig 19.8 are designed to give you help when typing code:

List Properties/Methods displays a dropdown list box in the Code window which gives you a range of possible properties and methods that are valid at this point as shown in fig 19.9.

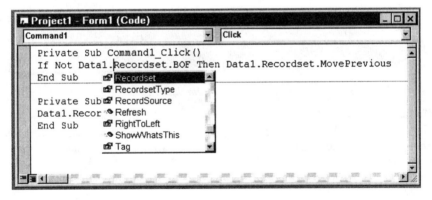

Fig 19.9 Displaying available properties and methods.

This is such a useful feature that you can enable it, so that it will appear without the need to choose this menu option repeatedly. To do this select the **Tools | Options** menu item and check the **Auto List Members** check box on the **Editor** page.

You can select one of the items displayed in the list box by selecting it using the up and down arrows and pressing the Tab key or by double clicking on the item you want.

List Constants performs a similar function, it displays a list of possible constants after you have typed an equal sign. If you enable the **Auto List Members** check box to display possible properties and methods, constants are also displayed where it is appropriate to the context of the code you are typing.

Quick Info gives you the syntax for a variable, function, method or procedure as shown in fig 19.10.

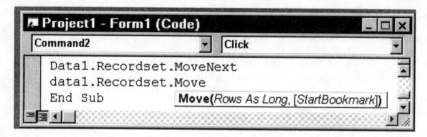

*Fig 19.10 Displaying the syntax for the **Move** method.*

To have this facility automatically enabled, select the **Tools | Options** menu and select the **Auto Quick Info** check box on the **Editor** page.

Complete Word types the remainder of the word you are entering when you have typed enough characters for Visual Basic to recognise the word.

Sometimes when you are editing the code in your application you may want to put a temporary mark in the code so that you can find that place again easily. The **Bookmarks** option, shown in fig 19.11, allows you to do this.

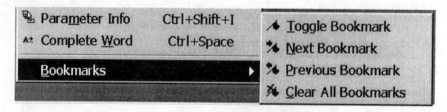

Fig. 19.11 Using bookmarks.

To add a bookmark to the current position in your code, click on **Toggle Bookmark**. If you click on this option at a place where there is an existing bookmark, the bookmark will be removed. You can clear all the bookmarks or move the bookmarks using the options shown. You can tell if there is a bookmark at a particular position by the presence of a small coloured square on the left of the text.

The View menu

One of the annoying problems with all current Window development environments such as Visual Basic is the proliferation of windows and files. It makes it difficult to find what you want. The **View** menu has been designed to help you.

Fig 19.12 shows the first part of this menu.

Fig. 19.12 *Finding text and objects.*

The **Code** option moves the focus to the current code window, the **Object** option takes you to the currently selected option. When you are working on a form at least one object always has the focus.

The **Definition** option moves the cursor in the code window to the place where the variable of procedure under the cursor is defined.

Last Position moves the cursor to the previous position in the code window. You can move to the previous six positions.

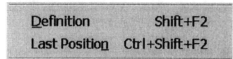

Fig. 19.13 *Moving to definitions and previous positions.*

The Object Browser is a key feature of version 5, which allows you to view objects and their events and properties.

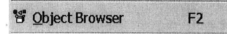

Fig. 19.14 *Finding the Object Browser.*

If you select the **Object Browser** option the window shown in fig 19.15 is shown.

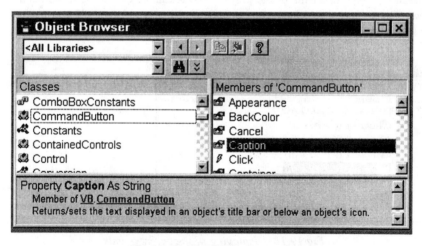

Fig 19.15 *The Object Browser.*

The Object Browser displays all of the classes in all the libraries in this example, however you can limit the scope, for example, to your project. All of the properties and event procedures for the currently selected class are also displayed with a brief explanation at the bottom of the window. In fig 19.15, the **Caption** property of the

CommandButton class is displayed. For a detailed discussion of classes and objects see chapter 12.

Fig 19.16 is used to display windows related to debugging, this is covered in detail in chapter 11.

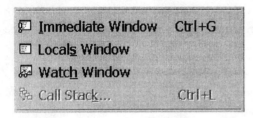

Fig. 19.16 Debugging options.

The Project Explorer is a key way of finding your way around the project. It allows you to move easily between components.

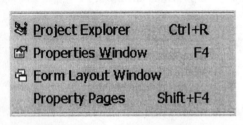

Fig. 19.17 Finding windows.

The Project Explorer has two types of display. The first is shown in fig 19.18. This shows all of the components of the project, and the name of the file in which they are stored. The folder which these components are in is not shown. If you click on the Toggle Folders button an alternative layout is displayed as shown in fig 19.19.

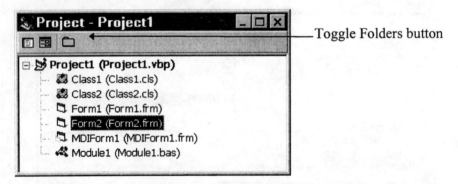

Toggle Folders button

Fig 19.18 Displaying project components.

Clicking on the View Object icon changes the focus to the selected object. The View Code icon changes focus to the code associated with the chosen object.

View Object button

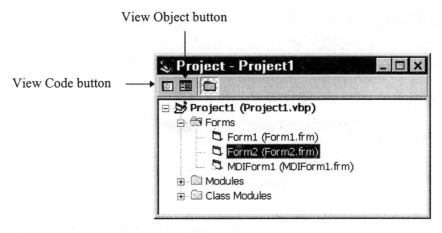

View Code button

Fig 19.19 Displaying project folders.

The **Toolbox** option displays the current configuration of the toolbox. This can be extended by adding custom controls.

Fig. 19.20 The toolbox and color palette.

The **Color Palette** option allows you to change the colour of objects at design time. The palette is shown in fig 19.21.

Background colour

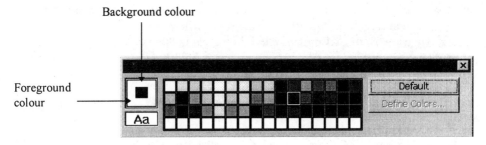

Foreground colour

Fig. 19.21 The Color Palette option.

To change the colour of a component:

- Select the component.
- Click on the background/foreground selector.
- Click on the colour you wish to choose.

The colour of text is the same as the foreground colour.

The **Toolbars** option is the last one on this menu and allows you to choose which toolbars are displayed. The toolbars are covered later in this chapter.

The Project menu

The **Project** menu is primarily concerned with project management and is covered in chapter 4, but there are a few useful facilities which have not been mentioned yet, in particular the **Project Properties** option. This consists of 4 tabbed pages. The **General** page is shown in fig 19.22.

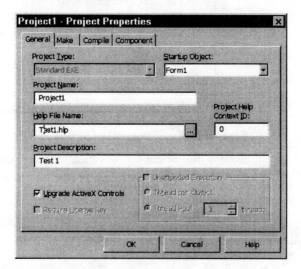

*Fig 19.22 The **General** page of the **Project Properties** option.*

The **Startup Object** is specified. This is usually the name of the first form to be displayed when the application starts. The default is *Form1*, the first form created.

If there is an associated help file its name is given here.

The **Upgrade ActiveX Controls** check box is set in this example. If a new version of an ActiveX control is found when the project is built it will replace the earlier one. This is particularly useful when upgrading an existing application to use 32-bit OCX rather than 16-bit VBX controls.

The second page shown in fig 19.23 is entitled **Make**. The most useful features are:

- The project title.
- The icon to be associated with this application. If a shortcut is created to this application in Windows 95, the specified icon will be used.
- The version number can be viewed and set to auto increment every time that the project is rebuilt.
- Information relating to this version can be created on this page.

The **Make** page also sets the attributes of the Visual Basic executable file. The major and minor version numbers and the revision version of the project are between 0 and 9999. If the **Auto Increment** option is selected the revision number is increased by one every time the **Make Project** command is given.

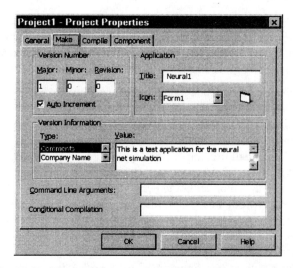

*Fig 19.23 The **Make** page of the **Project Properties** option.*

A **Title** for the project and an **Icon** can be specified.

The **Version Information** lets you specify information about the current release of your application.

Command Line Selection allows you to specify command line arguments which will be used when the application is run.

Conditional Compilation Arguments allow you to specify arguments for conditional compilation.

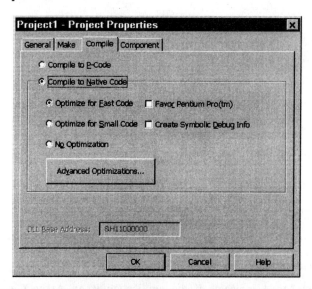

*Fig 19.24 The **Compile** page of the **Project Properties** option.*

The **Compile** page is shown in fig 19.23.

Compile to P-code produces p-code output.

Compile to Native Code produces Intel machine code for execution on a PC. You can specify some options depending on whether size or speed of the application is the most important and a few other characteristics of the executable application:

- **Optimize for Fast Code** - aims for an application which runs fast.
- **Optimize for Small Size** - aims for the smallest possible size of executable. There is usually a trade-off between speed and size.
- **No Optimization**. The optimisation process can take longer than the time taken to initially compile the application. Sometimes when you are developing the application and changing it a lot, you can save time by instructing the compiler not to perform any optimisation.
- **Favour Pentium Pro**. Optimise the code for the Pentium Pro processor. The application will run on earlier processors but will not execute fast.
- **Create Symbolic Debug Info**. Add symbolic debug information to the executable for debugging. If you use this option you can use any compatible debugger such as that found in Visual C++. A file with a PDB extension is created containing the debug information.

Advanced Optimizations displays a dialog box which allows you control over specific aspects of the optimisations.

DLL Base Address overrides the base address of 0X10000000 for a DLL file.

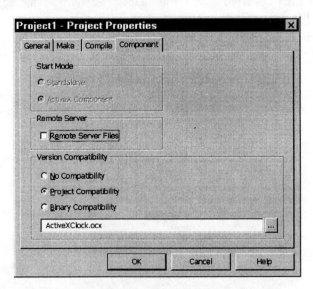

*Fig 19.25 The **Component** page of the **Project Properties** option.*

The **Component** page is shown in fig 19.25:

- **Start Mode** indicates if the application is an ActiveX component or a standalone application.

- **Remote Server**. This option is only available in the Enterprise version of Visual Basic. When selected it creates a VBR file which is needed by the Windows registry to run an ActiveX server on a remote computer. The VBR file has the same name as the created DLL file.
- **Version Compatibility** determines the degree of compatibility between this application and other versions of Visual Basic.
- **No Compatibility**, compatibility with earlier versions is not enforced.
- **Project Compatibility** allows you to select a project which this project is to be made compatible with. The project you select is displayed in the File Location text box near the bottom of the window. If this is cleared the File Location is disabled.
- **Binary Compatibility** is used to maintain compatibility between projects which use your ActiveX component.

The Format menu

All of the options on this menu list are concerned with organising controls on forms to give your applications a professional look. Few things look more amateur in a Windows application than controls which do not line up and have uneven gaps between them. The **Format** menu is shown in fig 19.26. Virtually all of these menu options have sub menus.

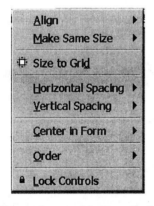

Fig 19.26 The ***Format*** *menu.*

The first option on this menu is **Align**, its sub menu is shown in fig 19.27. The first six of these options can only be used when more than one control has been selected.

To use the alignment options, select the controls you wish to align and choose how you wish them to be aligned. Controls are always aligned to the control nearest to the top of the form. If two controls are in the same vertical position, it is the leftmost control which all others are aligned to. To select more than one control, you can drag a dotted rectangle and enclose the controls you wish to select, or keep the **Ctrl** button pressed when you click on successive controls.

The last option **to Grid** is different to the previous options. As a default, forms are covered with a matrix of dots at design time. You can set an environment option so that controls will snap to the grid, that is so that the top left corner of a control is always on a grid point. If you drag a control and do not release it over a grid point, it will snap to the nearest. If you click on the **to Grid** option all controls will snap to their nearest grid point. You can control the spacing of the grid from the **Tools** menu, the **Options** option and the **General** page. This is covered later in this chapter.

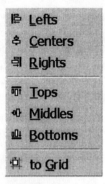

*Fig. 19.27 The sub menu of the **Align** option.*

Another key to making your applications look professional is to use the **Make Same Size** option to ensure that a selected groups of objects have the same width and height.

*Fig 19.28 The sub menu of the **Make Same Size** option.*

The **Size to Grid** option ensures that not only the top left corner of all selected objects are aligned with the grid, but all corners of it are on grid points. It does this by snapping each corner to the nearest grid point.

The Debug menu

The **Debug** menu is covered in chapter 11 which discusses debugging in detail.

The Run menu

If you want to start executing your application, you need to choose **Start** or **Start with Full Compile** from the **Run** menu, shown in fig 19.29.

The **Start** option runs the application, it will initialise all variables and display the start-up form. This command is only available at design time. Since you will be using this option a lot it is worthwhile using the shortcut key **F5.**

The **Start With Full Compile** option will completely build the application before starting to run. After building it behaves in the same way as the **Start** option. The shortcut key is **Ctrl+F5.**

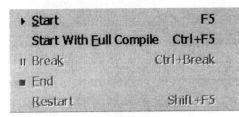

Fig 19.29 *The sub menu of the*
Make Same Size *option.*

The remaining three options are only available at run-time and are discussed in chapter 11 on debugging.

The Tools menu

The **Tools** menu is a mixture of facilities which do not really seem to fit together. The **Add Procedure** option is a useful shortcut way of adding a new procedure. It provides a suitable header depending on the type of procedure you wish to add to your code. The code window must have the focus for this option to be available. The procedure which is added is inserted at the current cursor position.

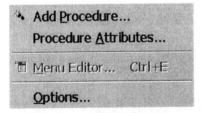

Fig 19.30 *The* ***Tools*** *menu.*

If you select the **Add Procedure** option you will see the dialog box shown in fig 19.31.

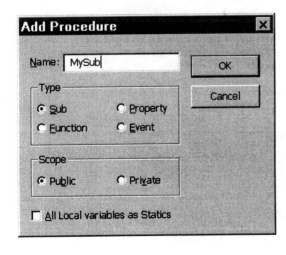

Fig 19.31 *The* ***Add procedure***
dialog.

In this example the code shown below is inserted at the current cursor position:

Public Sub *MySub( )*

End Sub

You have to add the code for this procedure within the template created. It is a good idea to use this command to avoid unnecessary typing which is a source of errors.

The **Procedure Attributes** option provides you with details about a specified procedure.

The **Menu Editor** option is used to create menus, this is covered in detail in chapter 14.

The **Options** option provides a detailed and complex set of facilities for controlling the Visual Basic environment. There are six pages:

- **Editor**.
- **Editor Format**.
- **General**.
- **Docking**.
- **Environment**.
- **Advanced**.

The Editor Page

The **Editor** page is shown in fig 19.32.

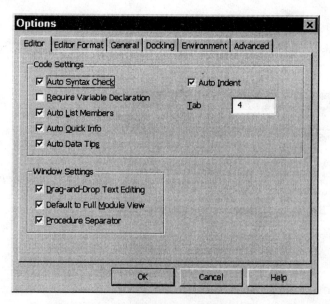

*Fig 19.32 The **Editor** page.*

The key features are:

- **Auto Syntax Check**. This checks the syntax of code. If this option is set and there is an error in the current line, a warning dialog is displayed when you attempt to move to another line. Even if this option is switched off, if there is a syntax error in a line of code, that line is displayed in a distinctive colour (the colour depends on the settings you have made in the **Editor Format** page of this option).

- **Require Variable Declaration** is an option which should be switched on if you are developing serious applications. If set this option requires you to declare any variables before using them. If you do not, an error is reported when you build your application.

- **Auto List Members** displays a list box containing options which would complete the statement.

- **Auto Quick Info** displays information about functions and function parameters.

- **Auto Data Tips**. When the cursor is clicked on a variable its value is displayed if this option is selected.

- **Auto Indent** will automatically indent lines in your code by one tab position after meeting reserved words such as for statements which mark the start of a block of code. If this option is not set all of your program statements will be aligned with the left margin which greatly reduces readability.

- **Drag and Drop Text Editing** if set, allows you to select code and then keeping your finger on the mouse button to move the code to a new position. This is a lot easier than using the menu or the toolbar icons for moving text.

- **Default to Full Module View** controls how much is displayed in the code window. If this is not set, only one procedure is displayed in the code window and you have to move between procedures using the drop down lists at the top of the code window. If this option is set the entire module is displayed. Most people prefer to work with this option set.

- **Procedure Separator** if set, displays a line marking the end of one procedure and the start of another in the code window.

If you want to change the font and colour of your code editor you need to use the **Editor Format** page.

The Editor Format Page

The features on this page, shown in fig 19.33 are straightforward. You have complete control over the colour and fonts used in the code editor.

As you select an item of text in the **Code Colors** text box, such as the **Comment Text** as shown, details of its colours and font are displayed, and you can change them as you wish. Visual Basic will apply a sensible set of colours depending on your Windows set-up, but you can use this page to do some fine tuning.

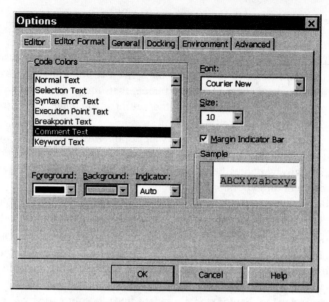

*Fig 19.33 The **Editor Format** page.*

The **Margin Indicator Bar** controls whether the margin indicator (the thick line on the left of the code window) is visible or not. It is recommended that you show this bar, since it makes it easier to turn breakpoints on and off.

The General Page

This group is a rather loose collections of unrelated items which does contain some important facilities. The grid settings are controlled from this page. The grid is shown at design time as a matrix of dots over the forms. You can control the following settings:

- **Show Grid**, determines whether the grid is displayed or not at design time, it is always invisible at run-time.
- **Width** and **Height**, the spacing between the grid points, a setting of 120 points for both seems to be sufficient.
- **Align Controls to Grid**, if this is switched on, the top left corner of all controls will snap to the nearest grid position. This is a useful feature, since it ensures that controls are aligned with each other to give a professional look to your applications.

It is unlikely that you would guess that the grid settings are controlled from this page or that the options concerning grids would be found on the same page as settings covering **Error Trapping** and **Compile** options.

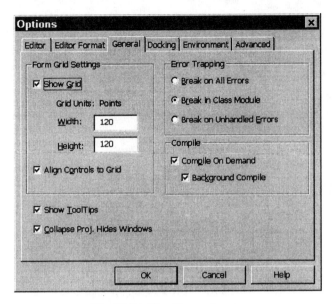

*Fig 19.34 The **General** page.*

There are three **Error Trapping** options:

- **Break on all Errors,** any error transfers control to break mode whether an error handler is active or not.
- **Break in Class Modules,** any error which occurs in a class module and is not handled causes the application to enter break mode.
- **Break on Unhandled Errors,** if an error occurs and an error handler is active, the error is trapped without going into break mode.

There are two compile options:

- **Compile on Demand,** if this option is checked a project will not be automatically re-compiled before being run.
- **Background Compile,** if this is set, idle time is used during run-time to finish compiling the application in the background. Selecting this option can reduce the compile time prior to running the application. This option is not active unless the **Compile on Demand** option is also checked.

The Docking Page

Docking is regarded by some users as being a very useful feature. If an object identified in the list on this page, (shown in fig 19.35) is checked that object can be docked at the top or bottom of the screen rather than remaining as a free floating window. Even if a window is dockable you can still drag it to a new position.

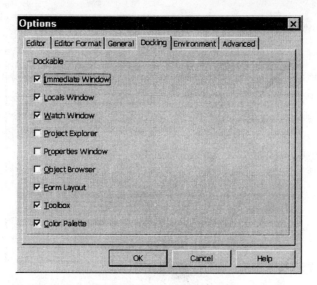

*Fig 19.35 The **Docking** page.*

It is worthwhile experimenting with these options to find a setting that suits you. The settings that I prefer are shown in fig 19.35.

The Environment Page

This page specifies some key attributes of your Visual Basic environment. It is shown in fig 19.36.

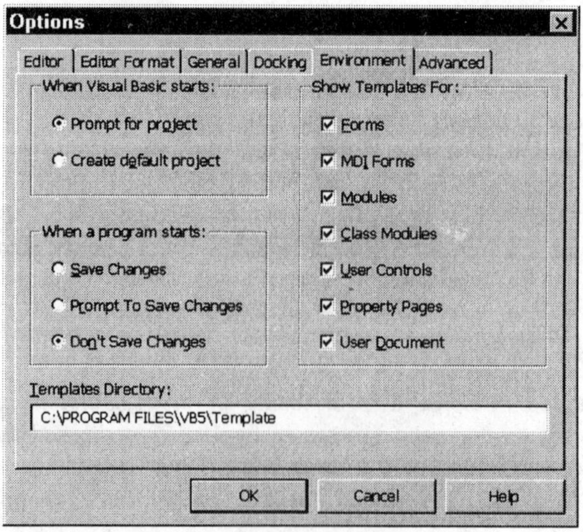

*Fig 19.36 The **Environment** page.*

There are four sections to this page:

- **When Visual Basic starts.** When you start a new project, you can either choose the type of project from a menu which prompts you to specify what the type of project is as shown in fig 19.37:

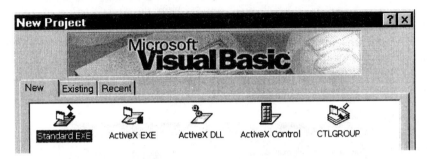

Fig 19.37 When Visual Basic starts.

You can also choose whether to open a new project, an existing one or one from a list of recently used projects. If you set **Create default project,** a new Standard EXE project is started rather than prompting for the project type when you run Visual Basic.

- **When a program starts.** When you start an application running it is sometimes helpful to automatically save any files in the project which have changed. You can specify if you wish changed files to be saved either with or without prompting. The default is **Don't Save Changes**. This is dangerous, since if your application crashes any changes you have made may be lost.
- **Show Templates for.** There are seven **CheckBox** controls in this section. If, for example, the **Forms** check box is set, when you add a form to your project using the **Add Form** option from the **Project** menu you will be prompted to specify if you wish to add a new form or an existing one. If the check box is not checked, a default new form will be added to the project. The **CheckBox** controls for other options such as **MDI Forms** and **Modules** behave in the same way.
- **Templates Directory.** This text box specifies the folder where the templates used in the other options on this page are stored.

The Advanced Page

There are three **CheckBox** controls on this page, shown in fig 19.38:

- **Background Project Load.** Controls whether code is loaded in the background or not. If this option is selected, control is returned to the programmer more quickly.
- **Notify when changing shared project items.** Two or more projects can share forms or modules. If they are modified in each project, when you leave

Visual Basic you will be asked if you wish to save all the components of the open projects including the shared items. If you do save the different versions of the shared items, the last version saved will overwrite all the earlier versions. If you select this option, whenever a shared item is changed, you will be asked if you wish to update all the other versions of the shared items to ensure that all open projects have the same version of the shared form or module.

- **SDI Development Environment.** If this check box is set the development environment changes from the default MDI (Multiple Document Interface) to an SDI (Single Document Interface). The MDI interface allows you to have more than one project open within the Visual Basic environment.

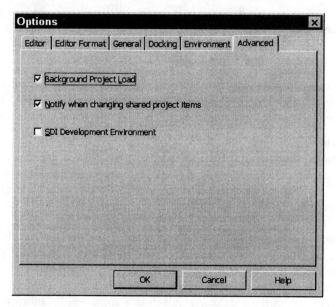

*Fig 19.38 The **Advanced** page.*

The Add-Ins menu

The **Add-Ins** menu is shown in fig 19.39.

*Fig 19.39 The **Add-Ins** menu.*

The **Visual Data Manager** is covered in detail in chapter 18 which deals with creating database applications.

The **Add-In Manager** is an OLE server that allows you to add additional capability to your Visual Basic environment, such as the Visual Data Manager and wizards which help you in the design of your applications. There are nine available wizards in the Professional release of Visual Basic as shown in fig 19.40.

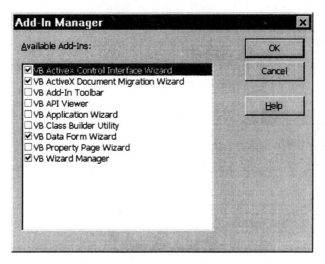

Fig 19.40 Visual Basic wizards.

The Window menu

The **Window** menu is shown in fig 19.41.

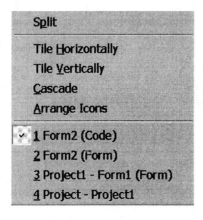

Fig 19.41 The **Window** menu.

This menu allows you to split a text window into two separate sections - each of which may be edited independently. This is useful if you are making changes to two parts of a file and do not wish to keep on scrolling up and down.

The **Tile Horizontally** and other options rearrange the open windows in the standard way.

All the available forms and code modules in the project are listed, and you can shift the focus to a window by clicking on its name.

The Help menu

The **Help** menu shown in fig 19.42 offers the usual excellent help facilities we have come to expect from earlier versions of Visual Basic.

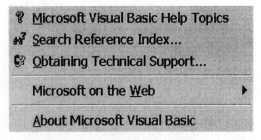

*Fig 19.42 The **Help** menu.*

In addition, in recognition of the increasing use of the World Wide Web, there is access to the Microsoft Web site which contains the most up to date information. The pages available are shown in fig 19.43.

Fig 19.43 Obtaining on-line help.

You do of course need an active Internet connection to use this facility.

The toolbars

There are 4 toolbars which provide a shortcut way of running the most frequently used functions without using the menu. As a default the standard toolbar, shown in fig 19.44 is displayed.

Fig 19.44 The menu and standard toolbar.

The other three menu toolbars can be displayed by selecting the **View | Toolbars** menu option as shown in fig 19.45.

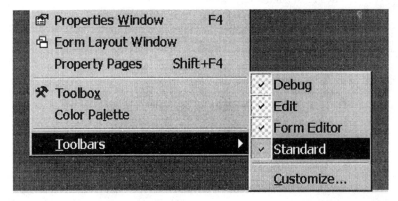

*Fig 19.45 The **Toolbars** option from the **View** menu.*

The standard toolbar

The standard toolbar contains six groups of buttons which are used for:

- Project and file management.
- Opening and saving projects.
- Editing.
- Undoing and re-doing actions.
- Running applications.
- Focusing on different windows in the environment.

The toolbar contains a set of commonly used commands which can also be invoked using the menu.

Project and file management

The standard toolbar is displayed by default although in common with the other toolbars, you can hide it from your desktop. This toolbar is different from the others covered in this chapter since it is not specific and has a range of unconnected functions, concerned with themes as diverse as adding forms to projects, starting the menu editor, editing and displaying different features of the environment such as the Properties window.

Table 19.1 Project and file management.

Button	Function	Equivalent menu command
	Add Standard EXE project. If you click on the arrow on the left of the button, the sub-menu shown below is shown which allows you to choose the type of project you want to add. 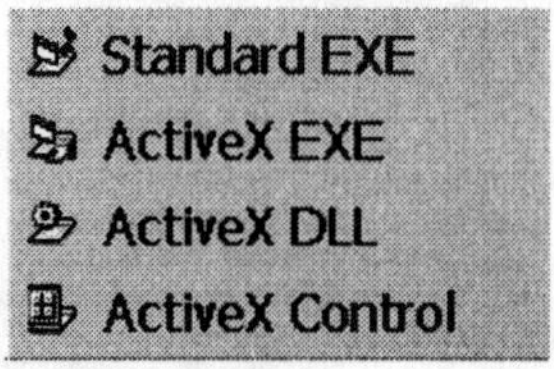	**File | New Project**
	Clicking on the down arrow displays a sub-menu which allows you to add a variety of objects to your project. 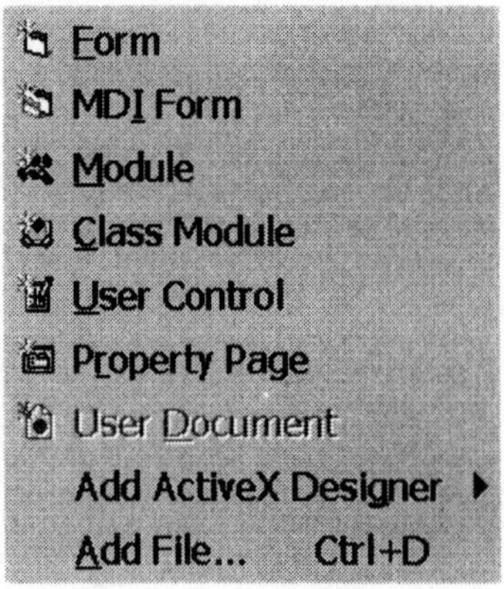	**Project | Add Form**

Displays the menu editor. **Tools | Menu Editor**

Opening and saving projects

Table 19.2 Opening and saving projects.

Button	Function	Equivalent menu command
	Closes the current project and prompts you to open a new project.	**File | Open project**
	Saves the current project and all associated files.	**File | Save Project**

Editing

Table 19.3 Editing.

Button	Function	Equivalent menu command
	Cuts the selected text or control and puts it in the clipboard.	**Edit | Cut**
	Copies the selected text or control and puts it in the clipboard.	**Edit | Copy**
	Pastes the contents of the clipboard in the current position.	**Edit | Paste**
	Displays a dialog box which prompts you for text to search for.	**Edit | Find**

Undoing actions

Table 19.4 Undoing actions.

Button	Function	Equivalent menu command
	Undoes the previous action.	**Edit	Undo** The name of the action to be undone is also given.
	Redoes the previous action if undo was the last command.	**Edit	Redo** The name of the action to be redone is also given.

Running applications

Table 19.5 Running applications.

Button	Function	Equivalent menu command
	Starts running the application.	**Run	Start**
	Stops a running program and enters break mode.	**Run	Stop**
	Stops a running program and returns to design mode.	**Run	End**

Focusing on windows

The buttons in this section of the toolbar help you to display different parts of the Visual Basic development environment.

Table 19.6 Focusing on windows.

Button	Function	Equivalent menu command
	Displays the Project Explorer.	**View	Project Explorer**
	Displays the Properties window.	**View	Properties Window**
	Displays the Form Layout window.	**View	Form Layout Window**
	Displays the object browser.	**View	Object Browser**
	Displays the toolbox.	**View	Toolbox**

The Debug toolbar

Debugging is discussed in chapter 11.

The Edit toolbar

The tools on this toolbar provide a set of functions which will assist you in writing code. A common problem when writing Visual Basic is to forget the exact syntax or the name of a constant value. This toolbar will help you with these difficulties. The bookmark facility is very useful when moving around your code.

Table 19.7 The Edit toolbar.

Button	Function	Equivalent menu command
	Displays a list box in the code window which lists the available properties and methods for the selected object.	**Edit	List Properties/Methods**

	Displays a list in the code window of the valid constants for the current property that you have typed.	**Edit | List Constants**
	Shows the syntax for a method, procedure or function at the current cursor position.	**Edit | Quick Info**
	Displays a pop-up window that shows information about the parameters of the procedure or function at the current cursor position.	**Edit | Parameter Info**
	Visual Basic completes the word you are currently typing.	**Edit | Complete Word**
	Moves all the selected text one tab position to the right.	**Edit | Indent**
	Moves all the selected text one tab position to the left.	**Edit | Outdent**
	Sets or clears a breakpoint at the current line.	**Debug | Toggle Breakpoint**
	Changes the selected text into comments.	No equivalent menu command.
	Changes comments into code by removing the comment character at the start of the line.	No equivalent menu command.

	Toggles a bookmark on the current line.	**Edit | Bookmarks | Toggle Bookmarks**
	Moves to the next bookmark.	**Edit | Bookmarks | Next Bookmark**
	Move to the previous bookmark.	**Edit | Bookmarks | previous Bookmark**
	Deletes all bookmarks.	**Edit | Bookmarks | Clear All Bookmarks**

The Form Editor toolbar

This toolbar provides a shortcut way of arranging the objects on a form, in particular so that they are correctly aligned with each other.

Table 19.8 The Form Edit toolbar.

Button	Function	Equivalent menu command
	Moves the selected objects to the front of other objects on a form.	**Format | Order | Bring to Front**
	Moves the selected objects behind all other objects on a form.	**Format | Order | Send to Back**
	Aligns selected components. There are seven possible options: leftmost edges are aligned, centre, right, tops, middles, bottom alignment and aligning the top left of the components to the closest grid.	**Format | Align**

Aligns the centres of the selected objects to a vertical line down the middle of the form.

Format | Center in Form

Adjusts all the selected components to have the same width.

Format | Make Same Size | Width

Locks and unlocks controls. When a control is locked it cannot be moved until it has been unlocked.

Format | Lock Controls

Index